LiT.

W9-CMM-173

Robert Sargent
1968

CARMELITE MONASTERY
LIBRARY
SARANAC LAKE, N.Y.

A LIVING LITURGY

A LIVING LITURGY

Reflections on the Liturgy and on Daily Life

by
PAUL CHAPEL, O.F.M.

Translated and adapted by
MARTIN W. SCHOENBERG, O.S.C.

NEWMAN PRESS
Westminster, Md.   New York, N.Y.   Glen Rock, N.J.
Amsterdam   Toronto

264.001
ChL

This book was originally published under the title *Gegeven Voor U* by St. Franciscus Stichting, Weert, Netherlands.

Nihil Obstat: Joseph A. Fichtner, O.S.C.
    Censor Deputatus

Imprimi Potest: Leo W. Kapphahn, O.S.C.
    Vice-Provincial

January 25, 1967

Nihil Obstat: William F. Hogan, S.T.D.
    Censor Librorum

Imprimatur: ✠ Thomas A. Boland
    Archbishop of Newark

August 8, 1967

The Nihil Obstat and the Imprimatur are official declarations that a book or pamphlet is free of doctrinal or moral error. No implication is contained therein that those who have granted the Nihil Obstat and the Imprimatur agree with the contents or with the opinions expressed.

Copyright © 1967 by
The Missionary Society
of Saint Paul the Apostle
in the State of New York

Library of Congress
Catalog Card Number: 67-28698

Published by Newman Press
Editorial Office: 304 W. 58th St., N.Y., N.Y. 10019
Business Office: Westminster, Maryland 21157

Manufactured in the
United States of America

Contents

CHAPTER ONE

Renewal of the Liturgy

Reactions and Difficulties

Vatican Council II gave the go-ahead sign for the *aggiornamento*, the updating, of the liturgy. The first steps toward bringing this about have been taken. The vernacular language is used more widely, and some of the ceremonies have been simplified. A beginning has been made.

Reactions, however, are not wanting. They run the full gamut from unbounded enthusiasm to utter dismay. Many are grateful that the eucharist especially is becoming meaningful for them. Others feel that the changes have disrupted their security. There are some who speak about vandalism and barbarism. Here and there one even finds people who are rebelling against these changes. The fact is that everywhere the subject is the center of conversation: in homes, in factories, in stores, even on buses, trains and planes. Alongside devoted supporters one finds everywhere also staunch opponents and disillusioned people, for whom it is particularly difficult to relinquish the old.

All this is readily understandable. It is especially hard for the many who worked with great zeal and intensity to identify themselves with the "old" liturgy, and who succeeded in doing so, albeit with much effort, so that the Roman missal became for them a reliable source of true spiritual nourishment. It can only be difficult for such people to renounce the wealth they so painstakingly acquired. Every separation is difficult but it is more painful in the measure that one has become attached to what must be given up. To have no regard for the plight of such people would indeed be a sign of liturgical shortsightedness and lack of feeling. On the other hand these people, too, must be willing to examine the new for its intrinsic value, taking into account at the same time the difficulties which the new must face.

This is particularly evident where the vernacular is concerned. One's own mother tongue will occasionally stumble and falter. But is that so remarkable? This is its first introduction to the Western liturgy. No wonder then that its bearing is somewhat uneasy; bashful people frequently spill coffee at table because they do not feel at home. We must grant our mother tongue liberal freedom and a fair amount of time to adapt itself to the liturgy. Whoever is critical in only a negative manner commits a pedagogical error to which many a child has been unfortunately subjected.

Among the objections which are raised against the new liturgy one frequently hears the word "chaos." Is this correct? It depends upon what is meant by the word. If one wants to say that experimentation is carried on everywhere in a totally irresponsible manner or, what is worse, in an unscientific manner for the sheer purpose of changing things, then indeed one must grant that chaos can result. Yet we know of no instance of such experimentation. One must not be too ready with condemnations and anathemas. On the other hand it cannot be denied that mistakes are being made. However, such is the case wherever there is authentic life. It is not hard to see how a pastor, who realizes that the liturgy has no meaning for a great part of his people, is seriously disturbed by this factor and seeks for means to make the liturgy something

meaningful for these people also. He will naturally run
the risk of following the wrong path. Whoever tries to
work will make mistakes. Whoever lives must take risks. If
one drives a car, he takes the risk of suddenly running
over a child. Does that mean that one must not drive a
car? Must one cease living? It is obvious that the mistake
of these pastors is much less serious than of those who in
total passivity let the whole thing ride and camouflage
their inertia under a smoke screen of so-called strict obedience. Whether this is actually the case is not the point
at the moment, though it is well to remember that the
letter kills and the spirit alone gives life. A legalistic
Christianity is doomed to perish through formalism. As
far as that is concerned, we may recall Christ's warning to
the Pharisees on this point.

It cannot be denied that this is a serious and difficult
situation. We feel everywhere the tension between law
and life. Naturally laws are necessary for an ordered existence. Yet, every law is something static, whereas life is
dynamic; a law is a fixation, whereas life is movement.
There comes the time when life bursts the bounds of law
just as a child outgrows his clothes. A certain law then
ceases to accomplish its purpose and must thus be changed.
The purpose of the law is always above its letter. This principle should be acceptable to all. Yet in practice this principle often causes great tension. That this
principle necessarily leads to chaos is difficult to see. That
it is the sign of an existing chaos we utterly deny.

Does all this threaten the unity of the Church? This
objection is also frequently made. "In this church things
are done this way; in another church they are done that
way." One should perhaps remark here that the differences are anything but essential. They consist chiefly in
the fact that in one church songs are being sung, the
priest greets his people, or possibly even omits the Introit,
while in the next church there is none of this. Look at it as

you please, but one can hardly speak of basic differences
which threaten the unity of the Church.

Some consider it disadvantageous that now, when trav-
eling in a foreign country, one is no longer so familiar
with the Mass as one was when, whether in Barcelona or
Berlin or Rotterdam or New York, the Mass was celebrated in exactly the same manner. But even here there is
no danger of loss of unity, simply because such unity
never existed. If such people were to attend Mass according to the Dominican rite or in a church of the Carmelites,
he would notice that something else was done. Yet he
would not call this broken unity. If one has expanded his
experience on a somewhat larger scale and become acquainted with other liturgies—as, for example, to mention
one of many, the Byzantine rite—he would see how radically different this liturgical celebration is from that of
the Western rite.

The only thing which one recognizes clearly at first
sight is the essence of every eucharistic celebration: the
proclamation of the Word and the breaking of the bread.
Yet no one will hesitate a moment about the union of the
Uniate Churches with the Church of Rome. Patriarch
Maximos of the Melchite Church rightly pointed out to
the Council fathers that it was not a question of introduc-
ing the vernacular into the liturgy of the Catholic Church,
since his Church was accustomed to use the vernacular.
"We are also Catholic," he added. The vernacular had to
be introduced only into the liturgy of the Western
Church. He even claimed that the usage of the vernacular
was one of the reasons why his Church continued to exist
and even to expand in spite of the fact that because of
persecution it had no Catholic schools, no organizations
or sodalities, no youth movements. The people learned to
know and to love their faith through the liturgy.

More serious, at least from the psychological point of
view, is the perplexity which leads many to unrest and

uncertainty. Such people experience every change as the overthrow of something absolute. Such disturbances can be digested occasionally, but if they continue or are repeated too often the structure of their faith begins to waver. They feel unsure and uneasy and thus unhappy. Where they had been taught that a chalice was never to be touched by unconsecrated hands, they now see how Mass servers and acolytes bring the chalice to the altar at the Offertory. Worse yet, they hear of parishes where the faithful receive the sacred species in their own hands, whereas formerly is was often said that one should not touch the sacred host even with one's teeth. No wonder then that such people ask: Isn't this bread really the body of the Lord? Possibly they have heard people speak in an unscientific and an untheological manner about the real presence of Christ in the sacrament and they were told— without the necessary explanations—that the Lord is present as a symbol. The question will then naturally arise whether the Lord is only symbolically present. With this question one of the most basic truths of the faith is placed in doubt for such people.

The bible is another point on which many people have suffered shocks. The story of creation, which was taught in school in precisely the manner as it is described in the first chapters of Genesis, seems now no longer to be either historical or scientific. The book of Genesis is plainly a religious book. It uses the form of a legend to tell how God created the world. This story naturally uses the thought patterns that were contemporary with the time of its origin: the earth is viewed as a large disc floating in the cosmos, the firmament as an enormous ceiling from which lights are suspended and in which there are openings which can permit the stored waters to descend in the form of rain. It is indeed quite possible that many confuse the literary form with the religious content and thus conclude that if the image of the disc is not correct, then the rest likewise will be mere fantasy. Such an inference is naturally false, yet we must take into consideration that there are people who do draw such conclusions. They find themselves still more confirmed in their opinion when their children come home from school and tell them that the narrative of Adam and Eve must not be taken too literally either. They are constantly subjected to such shocks.

In addition, in other areas connected with the liturgy there are adjustments which many find hard to accept. For example, not too long ago it was definitely suggested that one ought to go to confession before receiving holy communion. Holy communion was placed so far above the reach of the average sinful man that one dared approach the holy table only a few times a year after having gone to confession. Now one is told that the Lord associates with sinners as he did during his lifetime, and that the reception of holy communion is a means for having one's sins forgiven. It cannot be denied that this does cast a somewhat different light on the eucharist.

There are changes in the ethical field also. The rule of thumb which was used to measure the length of sleeves and skirts and trouser legs has been set aside. The scale which was used to weigh the ounces of a piece of bread on a fast day has also been shelved. There is a different view about the number of children a family should have. In like manner there is a different attitude toward the means by which a responsible spacing of children is to be accomplished. If twenty-five years ago a young married couple would have announced that from the very first they would strive for a responsible spacing of their children, they would have been roundly condemned. Now many are convinced that such measures are proper, if not obligatory. If in the past the instruction of the Church in the field of marital morality seemed to dwell particularly on its biological aspect so that many even formulated the axiom, "an offense against nature, therefore mortal," there is now the conviction that such norms are no longer acceptable. The instructions of the Church are being focused on a different aspect where she has indeed a serious and solicitous message. Her concern is no longer primarily with biology, but with love and with fellowship.

There is no doubt whatever that these emphases echo differently from what we were accustomed to. In a sense we are happy because of it. And yet it is readily understandable that these theories are shocking to many who were educated along different lines. Occasionally one even hears of complaints that one is being betrayed by the Church. All in all, it is also evident that these changes on the outlook of marital ethics are the cause of unrest and insecurity to many.

In order to make the litany of the causes of unrest and uncertainty more complete, we may point here to still another adaptation of man and his morality. Not too long ago a man was judged according to his concrete actions; now these concrete actions are judged according to the person himself, his background, his formation, his attitude. The result is that in the confessional less value is attached to an exact narration of all the concrete sinful actions, than to a manifestation of a man's sinfulness. Whoever can recall how formerly one strove painstakingly to give all the necessary details in the confessional, especially in matters concerning the sixth and ninth commandments, must admit that things have changed indeed.

Finally, we would like to point to the changes of attitude toward our separated brethren. Here, too, there has been development that can only be called healthy, but which causes uneasiness for many. Where formerly we held a strong polemic position against people of other faiths, we have now looked the Reformation squarely in the face and are beginning to recognize in it some of the features of Christ. This has been a mutual experience.

We have come to see that the Reformation also has a heritage from the Lord and that it has preserved certain heirlooms more carefully than we have. By way of example we may refer to the respect for and the acquaintance with the sacred scriptures. Likewise in matters of charity and aid to underdeveloped peoples, Christians of the various Churches have met and learned to respect each other.

Nevertheless one can detect among many a certain bitter resistance to such a rapprochement. How often does one not hear the remark: "It seems that we are gradually becoming Protestant." Such observations unfortunately betray an insufficient insight into the great differences which still separate the Christian Churches. One cannot help noticing how assertions are made precisely about nonessential matters. Thus one may hear criticisms when in a Catholic church those present are asked to sing a "psalm" or when it is said that the priest must "precede" the eucharist. These words seemingly arouse antagonisms which are really not to the point. Similar phenomena are experienced by ministers when they dare to light a candle at their service or if they ask those present to kneel. They are then told: "We are becoming much too Roman." It is really a pity that the movement toward Church unity is obstructed by emotional reactions. This is an unsound situation. If this unhealthy emotionalism is not controlled, there is danger that the ecumenical movement will lose momentum contrary to the expressed will of our Lord that we all be one. We may not remain divided or obstruct the effort toward reunion because of such trifles.

All in all it seems to us that with this summation, although incomplete, of facts, changes, and misunderstandings, we have clearly indicated why many find the renewal of the liturgy fraught with difficulties. It cannot be separated from renewal of other phases of the life of faith. It will be our effort in the following pages to remove the

difficulties and to lessen the objections by discussing the
background of the necessary renewal of the liturgy.

What Is the Liturgy?

Just what is the liturgy all about? What is it? That
there are misunderstandings on this point is plain to
everyone. One cannot deny that for many the word "liturgy" has an unsavory sound. One would be in for a few
surprises were one to conduct an opinion poll and ask
what people think of the liturgy. Many would indeed
have a definite opinion of their own. It is also possible
that there are many people for whom the term "liturgy"
has merely accidental connotations, such as a black edge
on a mourning card or a silver or golden edge on a jubilee
card. These are called "liturgical." Others will associate
the word "liturgy" with incense, candles and Gregorian
Chant, or with such bodily movements as rising, kneeling,
sitting, bowing, striking one's breast, answering prayers
and singing songs.

All this has precious little to do with the liturgy. Even
the introduction of the vernacular into the liturgy is far
from reaching the heart of the matter. This is only a
means for arriving at authentic liturgy. Furthermore, it
should be easy to see that all the bishops of the entire
world would not assemble in a council merely to talk
about the colors of the chasubles or about community
singing, while at the same time the whole world was
being consumed by a frightening conflagration. When two
thousand bishops speak for weeks on end about the liturgy, one is justified in presuming that they are concerned
about a topic which is of equal importance with peace,
disarmament, aid to underdeveloped nations or the unity
of Christianity. Not only is the liturgy as important as all

these other subjects, but it is also one of the possible means of bringing these world problems nearer to solution.

The Greek words *leiton ergon* when translated literally mean both "a service in behalf of the people" and "a service performed by the people." Looked at from this point of view one is really engaged in the liturgy when he sets himself to combat the hunger that prevails in the world. It was also authentic liturgy when millions of young men gave their lives for the freedom of the world in 1945; this was truly a service on behalf of the peoples of the world.

The things that happen in our churches on Sundays appear to have little connection with all this. There the liturgy gives the impression of being a sort of court ceremonial, a reenactment of an archiac ritual. It is admittedly difficult to see in it a service directly in behalf of the community, a service to each other, a service to the world. At first sight it appears, to say the least, very questionable how this liturgy can be a positive contribution to the solution of the problems that beset the world.

The Contrast between Liturgy and Life

Perhaps we have here one of the more basic reasons for a discrepancy which has grown between liturgy and life. That there is such a divergence cannot be denied. For many, attendance at Sunday Mass means little more than the fulfillment of an obligation, alongside with and independent of many other obligations. People have their duties as father or mother, as student or employee, as neighbor or friend, as a businessman or as a member of a family; in addition to this, "being a Catholic" also brings with it the obligation of celebrating the eucharist. That there is an inner connection between all our other obligations and this particular one escapes many. One cannot avoid the impression that for many going to church is something totally different from all the rest, something for which one must separate himself entirely from everything else. Thus one can occasionally hear someone say: "I will go to the early Mass because I can then go quickly to work."

It is our personal conviction that the celebration of the eucharist should instead be a concentrated experience, directed expressly toward God and toward each other, of our daily lives with all its earthly responsibilities, cares and readiness to serve. This is the way it should be. Yet a lot of water will flow under the proverbial bridge before the eucharist will be such a living reality to all who are present. The renewal of the liturgy indeed faces an enormous task.

Perhaps this discrepancy between liturgy and life is connected with the divergence which our thinking has established between God and the world, and between the divinity and the humanity of Jesus Christ. It will be helpful toward the solution of the problem which is now preoccupying us to direct our attention toward these disagreements which are the occasion for several basic misunderstandings.

Christ is God and man. But how are we to imagine this? The Council of Chalcedon has already given us an answer: "one person in two natures." But the questions remain: How are we to imagine this in the actual Lord Jesus? How are we to experience this in him? Just who was Christ? How did he appear? Many will call to mind Christmas sermons wherein they were told how the divine child lay in a manger as an ordinary human infant just like every other child. Preachers with a little more imagination would describe how the little child in the crib gurgled and drooled, just like any other baby. And then they would add immediately, almost as if the preacher himself were shocked by the idea, that Jesus did this only as man. As God he naturally did not gurgle with delight or drool. But everyone felt that here something strange was being added. Here there would be a duality in Christ which seems inhuman.

The problem is felt even more urgently when the evangelist says of Jesus that he increased in wisdom and stature with God and man (Lk. 2, 52). We immediately correct the expression of the evangelist by saying that he grew in wisdom only as man; as God he naturally knew everything.

Nor is the question less urgent when Christ, speaking to his apostles about the end, says that this all-important hour is not known even to the Son but only by the Father (Mt. 24, 36). Here, too, we are quick to correct the Gospel by adding that Christ was saying this as man; as God, he surely knew when the hour would come. But all along one feels an inclination to become irritated and ask: Did Jesus know, or didn't he? This division in his person makes us think of a split personality, a sort of schizophrenia, or even of deceit. Yet none of these suppositions may be made of Christ. Professor Schoonenberg, S.J., formulated this problem quite pointedly during the course of a liturgical conference held at Stoutenburg (Holland) during the week of Pentecost, 1965. He stated that the divinity and humanity in Christ are not competing with each other, nor can they be sharply separated. What is divine need thus not be less human. Furthermore, the Synoptic Gospels know of no such division. They do not call Christ one person with two natures but the Son of man, the Messiah. It is only in the Greek manner of thinking (which is also our manner of thought) that such a division is made.

One of the great merits of recent theology, also called the new theology, is that, mindful of the sacred scriptures and the primitive Church, it is seriously seeking to rephrase the unity of Christ. Christ's divinity does not give him something wholly strange in total opposition to his humanity. His divinity is rather the supporting basis of his manhood, of his humanity. It is precisely his divinity that makes him the unique man, the man par excellence, with a profoundly human understanding and a profoundly human wisdom. His inclination to forgive is unique but not inhuman; his divine disposition to forgive reveals him as the ideal man. His divine openness to the needs of others is a human openness, to crown all. That he permitted himself to be anointed by a publicly known sinful woman—particularly in that era—is a manifestation of his absolute humanity. Here his divinity is not competing with his humanity; rather his divinity makes him wholly man.

As we have already said, the Synoptic Gospels make no division between his divinity and humanity. In like manner there should be no such division in us when we receive the divine life through Christ. This divine life must not make us strangers to the world; on the contrary, it must make us more humane.

Similarly the relationship between God and his world must not be represented as an opposition. God is not a being who can be numbered in our world. He is not a being separate and apart from our world. He is rather the all-present and the all-supporting basis of the world. God is wholly in his world.

This has always been the teaching of God's omnipresence. At the same time it must be granted that it is now becoming difficult to pray in the liturgy: "Lord, teach me to despise the world." Naturally the word "world" is used here in a pejorative sense, referring to the world insofar as it is subject to sin. In view, however, of the intimate relationship between God and his world as we now know it, this is not the first nor the immediate signification of the word "world."

Unity must also be restored between the liturgy and life. Discrepancy is no more tolerable here than between the divinity and the humanity in the person of Christ.

In order to understand what liturgy really is and to see

how the liturgy is one with life, it is well to reflect on the liturgy of Bethlehem, Calvary and Tabor. There we have liturgy in its full expression. There Christ, the man par excellence, renders a priceless service to God and to man. It was liturgy when he became man in order to reestablish in us unity with God. It was liturgy when he proclaimed the Good News, healed the sick, comforted the poor, improved the righteous and exposed the hypocrites. It was liturgy when he was scourged for our sins in order that we might be healed through his stripes (Is. 53, 5). It was also liturgy when he rose from the dead and ascended to the Father to prepare a place for us (Jn. 14, 2-3). One can summarize it all by saying that on the one hand the liturgy of Jesus Christ is the homage which he brought to the Father and in which he also included us; on the other hand it is also his service to the community, to his fellowmen, which can never be equaled by us.

It is obvious that all this, this noble and yet basic humanness, has nothing to do with the form of a chasuble or the color on the edge of a mourning card. It should also be obvious that in the eucharist we have an authentic liturgy in the most etymological sense of the Greek word. In the liturgy of the Word, Christ proclaims his Good News; in the liturgy of the meal, he offers himself in love to the Father and to us. Looking at it in this way, we also receive new insight into the question of our active participation in the liturgy of Jesus Christ. Whoever is a recipient of this service will understand that a similar service is demanded of him. Truly active participation will then not consist in singing along, or in standing or kneeling, but in being of service to God and to fellowman, in expending all one's effort to establish peace in one's surroundings, to satisfy the hunger of as many as possible, to bring solace to others in one form or another. If this degree of active participation is not attained, one should seriously ask oneself if the eucharist was truly celebrated. All the rest of "active participation" makes sense only when it introduces us to active participation in the liturgy of Jesus Christ.

Vatican Council II requested that the liturgy be renewed and reformed. This undoubtedly means that more room must be made for the vernacular and that the rites be made more meaningful to our circumstances. It is also obvious that these changes are only means to induce those present to a more active participation. All these changes have as their goal to invite all the participants to a greater service of God and to more intensified service of their fellowman. It is only when this has been accomplished that the renewal may be termed successful because then the bond between liturgy and life, between service of God and service of man, between our duties as men and as Christians, has been reestablished.

Much of this has been lacking in the manner in which the liturgy has been celebrated until now. Many are compelled to acknowledge that the liturgy has not as yet deeply concerned them or moved them to a greater love of their fellowman. Until now they have experienced the tie between liturgy and life only in a small degree. Renewal has as its goal the strengthening of this relationship.

If the Church succeeds in this enterprise, then the liturgy can indeed become meaningful in our earthly responsibilities such as preserving the peace, reestablishing Christian unity and alleviating the plight of the world. This will really be the greatest service which Christians can offer to God and man. In short, active participation in the liturgy of Jesus Christ can mean nothing else than service to God through service to fellowman.

Implicit and Explicit Worship

Every service offered man, every exercise of earthly responsibility, is a service to God. It should be stated that working in a garden is serving God. For all things are from him and in him and through him. He is the ground-of-being of all that is. Everyone knows that we please a father by loving his child. This is true even here on earth, where the bond between father and child is somewhat loose and external when compared with the tie between God and his creatures and between God and his children. We must therefore conclude all the more certainly that every service done to one of God's children or to God's world is a service to God precisely because the link is so intimate.

Yet it would be risky to stop at this point. If service of God were to consist only in service of man, there would be great danger that in the long run we would lose sight of God and no longer realize that service of man is service of God, for service of God is worship. We would arrive at a sort of religious atheism. For this reason it is necessary from time to time to take a closer view of the third dimension, namely, the relationship of our lives to God.

This is something wholly human. Obviously this relationship exists at all times. Children love their parents all year long. Yet there is need of celebrating Mother's Day or Father's Day just to make sure that this love is not forgotten on the other days. All year long parents love and care for their children. Yet if they want to do this consciously, then they must give this love extra expression on certain days, a birthday for example. Married people are always in association with each other. He, the husband, works for the wife, and she works for him. The danger, however, is not excluded that they may forget this if they only implicitly express their regard for each other by working for each other. Both of them have a great need from time to time to express their mutual love explicitly. Beauty lies before us wherever we look. But a man who does not occasionally pay explicit attention to what is beautiful by admiring it in nature, in a museum, in a work of art, in a building, or wherever it may be found, will in

the long run no longer see beauty in the things that sur-
round him.

The same is true for the liturgy as worship. It is absolutely necessary that man periodically give explicit expression to the divine dimension of his life. There is an
absolute need for an external expression and experience of
this God-ward-ness of his life, of his earthly responsibilities and of his full humanity. It is necessary that in the
liturgy a *close-up* be made of all this, that a man consciously bring honor and love to God as the source of all
good, the Father of unending majesty, the infinitely Holy
One.

This third dimension reaches its acme in the eucharist.
There Christ is in the full service of his Father as no one
has ever been in his service. There Christ acts not as a
solitary individual, but as the man par excellence in con-
junction with all men. We are therefore included. We
stand together with Christ in the service of the one Father. When Christ surrenders himself so totally and so
lovingly to his Father, the man who is united with him
surrenders himself in like manner. The whole life of
Christ can be summarized in the first word attributed to
him by Paul: " . . . a body thou hast prepared for me. . . . I
have come to do thy will, O God" (Heb. 10, 5-7). It was
also his last word: "Into thy hands I commit my spirit"
(Lk. 23, 46). This was the motif of his entire life. In this
manner he gave explicit expression to the third dimension
of his life, his God-ward-ness.

It is helpful to exercise external worship as a special
close-up of this dimension. We may assert that God is
honored always wherever men are available to each other.
But when this implicit service of God is not made explicit,
there is the danger that it will sink into sheer humanism.
It will not become unreal, but it will lack its basic reason
and its strongest stimulus. The point is not that during the
time of the eucharist God's greatness and characteristics

are paraded before him. There is yet another way of praising which is really far more exalted—if one is truly happy because one has discovered the beautiful and the joyful in God. And this is to say a lot, so much in fact that in the eucharistic prayer we dare to say: "Lord, we thank you for the sacred passion, resurrection and glorious ascension of your Son. Because of this we offer your exalted majesty your own gifts as a pure and unstained sacrifice. . . . Through him, Lord, accept and sanctify these gifts. . . . Through him and with him and in him may all glory be to you. . . ."

The Worship of God and the Service of Man

There was a time when Christians thought they had to flee the world so as to be able to find and serve God in a place far from men. This type of spirituality does not appeal to us in our age. It seems not to have been Christ's standard either. He accomplished his ideal most perfectly when with his body he bound together two beams, the one in a vertical position, the other in a horizontal one; in other words, one beam which was pointing from earth to heaven, and another which was pointing from left to right —from man to man. We might say that he joined his divine love with his human love. He manifested his love for God by dying for his fellowmen. He offered himself to God by giving himself to his neighbor. In his love for God he did not flee from men. On the contrary in his love for the Father he sublimated the love for man. He did not flee the world; he came into the world.

The liturgy is being renewed. If there is something that must be changed in the liturgy, and which will be changed, then it is its unearthly, its unreal, its unworldly character. If the liturgy is not given an intimate relationship with our human need and our human desires, with our human life and our earthly responsibility, then the liturgy will remain something taking place in a void, where there are some vague allusions to redemption and forgiveness, but which has no contact with daily life. Liturgy means worship of God and service to men in compact unity, just as the two beams of Jesus' cross formed a unity.

If Christ put an end to any one thing, then it was to the division between religion and the regard for fellowmen. He served God most by serving men best. Christ never chose, nor was he ever compelled to choose, between God and men. He united God and men. He expressed his love for God in a most striking manner by dying and rising for men.

What was true of him also applies to us. We shall never be able to serve God unless we serve our fellowmen; we shall never be able to do a favor to God unless we do it to our fellowmen. The same thing was expressed positively by Christ when he said: "So if you are offering your gift at the altar, and there remember that your brother has something against you, leave your gift there before the altar, and go; first be reconciled to your brother" (Mt. 5, 23f.). Christ protested vehemently against the so-called religious practices of those who left their parents in need because they preferred to give their gift to God (Mk. 7, 11). And to those who still did not get the point he said: "As you did it to one of the least of these my brethren, you did it to me" (Mt. 25, 40). One must not regard this as a figure of speech or a legal fiction. These words of Jesus must be taken seriously. We may not choose between God and man. Whoever enters the Church to serve God cannot leave his fellowman outside. A liturgy which has no concern for man in need is radically rejected and irrevocably dismissed by God.

In Christ we find a clear example of how the worship of God is effected in the service of men. There is no question about it. It is God's plan and his desire that man be happy. We cannot serve him better than by devoting ourselves to make this plan and desire of God a reality. If men do not serve each other, they are disrupting God's plan. In that case they are not following his desire and responding to his command. When men do not serve each other, they abandon each other, they destroy each other, they confine each other into solitude and make each other unhappy. Recent history has shown beyond question that a world which is the victim of unbridled selfishness, of racial discrimination, of divisions, of concentration camps and gas chambers, and of hatred ends in disruption—and this is certainly not what God had in mind.

Where selfishness is mistress there can be no happiness in marriage, no peace in the family, no tolerance toward others, no willingness to help, no joy. And it is precisely God's desire, his plan, that there be peace and joy and happiness and well-being. His plan is that we help him create a new world of peace and happiness and love. We must not deceive ourselves into thinking that there is prayer or liturgy where there is no love of neighbor. Liturgy can only be effected when all these other elements are present.

There is thus no choice between God and man. Worship of God is intimately united with service of man. This is the basic reason why our liturgy may not be a stranger to the world, an ecstatic enjoyment of God, overlooking fellowman. For this reason the future liturgy may not be divorced from life. It would be a tragic oversight to think that we can withdraw from life for a while to worship God in a church. Our Sunday liturgy may not under any circumstances be something apart from our daily lives. Thinking to fulfill one's Sunday obligation without love of neighbor is sheer fancy.

In fact it is our principal task to incorporate the liturgy in a realistic manner into our entire lives. This is a must.

No greater catastrophe could happen to Christianity than that our worship should become an affair of the salon without any contact with the world. If our liturgy does not exert a positive influence on the world, then it simply is not liturgy.

It is remarkable that there are people who would not be at all offended if one were to tell them that they are "irreligious." There are even circles in which it is a sort of compliment to call one irreligious, as this would imply that this man is so cultured that he is able to do without the myth of religion. In his view religion was a temporary phenomenon in an age preceding our technological era. In his view it was only natural that primitive man, who was not yet able to help himself because of his defect in technological skills, would seek security from a higher source. He therefore created for himself a god in his own image and likeness; he imagined that this god was very powerful and could supplement the deficiencies of helpless man. According to the new technological man, this god no longer exists and religion serves no purpose.

In fact this imaginary god never existed. When irreligious people refuse to acknowledge this god, we can only agree with them and say that we also want nothing to do with this fanciful god.

But if one regards true religion as primitive magic one has missed the point. This can easily be seen from casual pieces of conversation which one hears from the lips of such irreligious people: "I don't go to church, but I am good to everyone; I do no one any harm; I deceive no one; I cooperate with the efforts to combat hunger; I do not see how I would be better if I were also religious." In other words these people affirm that they do not consider religion necessary in order to be good and to live fully human lives. Somewhere along the line there is a basic misunderstanding which prevents them from seeing that religion and love of neighbor stand and fall together. Authentic, perfect, complete, disinterested love of neighbor finds its deepest expression when it is paired with authentic religion. It must be admitted that occasionally this insight is wanting even among churchgoing people and that one may correctly reprove them that they do indeed go to church faithfully but have little influence on their fellowmen.

Why is true love of neighbor possible only in authentic religiousness? First we must say that man as he came from God's creative hand is bound by every fiber of his being to his fellowmen. It is not only a child who cannot live without father and mother; no man can live without his fellowmen. It is God's purpose that every man should be happy, but to be happy without love and appreciation is impossible. To be man, therefore, is to be social.

It is also evident that we cannot honor God in a better way than by helping to realize his plan, which is to make men happy. In this sense one must also say that every act of charity toward one's neighbor, even toward a so-called irreligious man, is implicitly a religious act.

In this same sense we must say that sin makes us not only irreligious but also uncharitable. Whoever sins—and this is true of every sin—fails in his concern for his fellowmen. Whoever sins is therefore inhuman in a certain sense, because to be human means to be social. Sin causes division; sin effects separation; sin divides men; sin disrupts. To be human means to be together, to seek fellowship, communication, association, love. To be human is an invitation to love, to be concerned about another. A sinful man is inhuman, a *no-man*.

There is something else. God became man. What this means is still far from clear to us. We are only gradually beginning to discover what the incarnation really means. In any event God became our fellowman in Christ. As we reflect on the life of Christ we become aware of his humanness. It was precisely this humanness which attracted people to Christ. He who chose to follow the way of the cross freed the widow of Naim from such a way. He who took all sins upon himself, and because of them was despised and rejected, seeks our sinners in their misery (Is. 53). He opens the eyes of the blind. He cleanses lepers. He befriends outcasts. He does not break the broken reed. He seeks the lost sheep. He is ready to forgive beyond our fondest expectations. He is truly human par excellence.

This service in behalf of mankind is continued in the liturgy. Our active participation in the liturgy then means that this helpfulness to mankind is continued through us. It is very clear that a Christian is not a sort of duality. A Christian is not man-and-Christian. A Christian is just a good man. A Christian is a man who has been redeemed and sanctified by Christ, which is to say he is a renewed man because of the example, the effective example, of the Lord. He becomes more a man because of the divine life within him. A good Christian is therefore a good man *per se*. To be a Christian means to be foremost a social man, because a Christian has been incorporated into the fellowship of Christ, the People of God. For this reason the hallmark demanded of a Christian, by which, according to our Lord, he is to be recognized, is that love dominate his relationship with his fellowman.

In the liturgy a man appears before God in company with Christ and his people. This presupposes a togetherness, a unity. This excludes egoism and individualism. Whoever partakes in the liturgy proclaims by this fact that he belongs to the fellowship of Christ, and the basic law of this fellowship of Christ is love. The communal homage of love and worship is something vain and futile if fellowship is a meaningless and empty word. This communal homage presupposes more than simultaneously occupying the same space. It presupposes an inner living unity which expresses itself in mutual love and concern.

On the other hand the liturgy also effects this unity. The liturgy makes us one. In the liturgy we literally expose ourselves to the same saving deeds of our Lord. It is this which makes us one People of God. Whoever truly participates in the liturgy experiences the presence of the Lord which binds us with him and with others in love.

The Notion of God in the Liturgy

In this chapter on the renewal of the liturgy we must not fail to say something about the notion of God in the liturgy. Whenever we come in contact with God in the liturgy, our idea of him must be as precise as possible. We will never succeed here on earth to form a picture of God that will in any way approach his reality, yet some of the lines are sketched by revelation. Sacred scripture permits us to see two characteristics of God in an admirable combination and unity. On the one hand it shows him to us as majesty personified; on the other hand he is depicted as a caring father. Sometimes God is even described as a mother who cherishes her children.

His majesty was revealed to Moses. Moses asked to see God's face. But Yahweh answered resolutely: "You cannot see my face, for man shall not see me and live" (Ex. 33, 20).

In his bitter sufferings Job reproached God and demanded he be told why he had to suffer so, but God could not tolerate such an attitude in Job. God's answer compelled Job to return to his proper station. God asked him where he got the right to tell God what to do. Almost sarcastically God asked Job whether he was counsellor at the creation of the world. Trembling before God's majesty Job answered: "Behold, I am of small account; what shall I answer thee? I lay my hand on my mouth. I have spoken once and I will not answer; twice, but I will proceed no further" (Job 40, 3-5).

In his relationship to God, man may never forget that

he is a creature. This means that everything God does for man is pure benevolence. God is not obligated to say "thank you" to any man. We are wholly and entirely God's. We exist because he wants us to. He is the sovereign majesty. We cannot comprehend him. And if we think we comprehend God, then we may be certain that we really do not understand what God is.

This, however, does not complete the image of God. Before the face of such a God, a man could only be frightened. There is more to be found in the sacred scriptures. There is a word which gives the image of God a much more complete aspect. This word is "Father." It gives a new hue to God's sovereignty; it adds a tint of boundless love to his majesty. It sketches a smile on his face. Yet there is more. The fatherhood of God is not something that has simply been added on; it is his very essence. Because of his fatherhood he can understand the weakness of men, he can listen to their afflictions, he can be merciful to failing man. Fear becomes reverence. Dread becomes love. Our trembling before him becomes a longing for him. Regardless of what he may permit to happen to us, of what he determines about or for us, we know that because of the word "Father"—which is only a slight indication of his real fatherhood—we will never suffer *because of* his hand but always *in* his hand. He will himself wipe away the tears from the eyes of those who come to him in their sorrows (Apoc. 7, 17; 21, 4). He himself told us that he does not desire the death of a sinner, but his conversion (Ezek. 18, 23). He also tells us that we must not be anxious about our food or clothing (Lk. 12, 29).

It is difficult to say what is uppermost in the liturgy—whether fear in the presence of God's omnipotence or confidence in his goodness. In the liturgy we see how both have been harmoniously joined. Here love is reverential and confidence respectful. Here intimacy is never brash nor openness bold. On the contrary there is respect and love, reverence, tact, nobility and confidence. This authentic notion of God is expressed when we pray: "We praise you, we adore you, we worship you, we glorify you, we give you thanks for your great glory." This authentic notion of God expresses itself in our gratitude toward him, who has been so benevolent to us in his Son. It makes us feel humble in his presence and we stammer: "Receive, O Almighty God, these offerings from us, your unworthy servants." We strike our breasts in repentance and say: "Have mercy on us." This notion of God becomes unutterable and we can only say: "Holy, holy, holy!" At the same time, however, this notion of God is filled with unshakable confidence in the majesty of God, our Father.

CHAPTER TWO

The Solemn Entrance

The beginning of our eucharistic celebrations at the present time still gives an impression of disorderliness. It consists of an accumulation of opening ceremonials which really obscure the opening. There is, or there was, the ceremony of the Asperges. Then the priest enters again, accompanied by the saying or singing of the Introit, the Confiteor, the Kyrie and the Gloria—each in turn a remnant of a preparation or an opening. The Collect following the invitation to prayer is really the beginning proper. We hope sincerely that the renewal which is to come will also bring some order and simplification in the opening of the service. On the other hand we hope that strict uniformity will not be prescribed. Let there be room for variation and adaptation suitable to the occasion and special circumstances.

On certain occasions a solemn entrance of the priest and his assistants appears very much in order. This is an element of the "old liturgy" which will retain its value for feast days. It is worth noting how often the Introit-hymn is a song of welcome addressed to Christ the Lord, whose coming among his own is depicted as the entrance of the priest. By way of example we may mention: "Rise up, O Lord, come to our aid"; "To you, O Lord, I lift up my soul"; "See, here he comes, the Lord, the ruler"; "The earth is full of God's glory"; "Hear, O Lord, my voice as it cries to you."

This exemplification and experiencing of the coming of the Lord among his people can have a meaning that is very salutary for many people. Without Christ we can do nothing; whoever expects everything from himself is going to fall short. It is only a short step from presumption to despair. This is perhaps the greatest temptation of our time—to give up hope. How frequently is it really the case that men turn their backs to God and to the Church because they have lost courage. Then one can hear them say: "I can't reach her requirements anyway, I cannot be loving, I cannot be pure; what is the use then of acting piously in church while I am not living accordingly in my daily life." The central point of all this discussion is the "I"; this is expected to do everything. But Christ said: "Without me you can do nothing." Even in a good confession the confessor hears the penitent say: "I am afraid that not everything is in order, that I have forgotten something of my former life, that I did not confess something correctly or that I was not sufficiently sorrowful." Here again the "I" stands in the center. Naturally the "I" forgot something or was not as detailed on a certain point as it might have been, for the simple reason that "I" is not infallible. This can be readily seen in daily life, as when someone goes out to run some errands, and then, having come home, discovers he forgot to bring along some sugar. It is to be expected that similar omissions will occur in the religious life. Christ asked us to have confidence in him. He is the cornerstone on which we may build confidently.

It is therefore reasonable to set the "I" aside a bit so as to make room for Christ. Without him we can do nothing; we can't pray, or love, or make an offering, or even approach God. No one is able to go to the Father except through him. The history of religion tells us of the strange and vain efforts which man has undertaken to reach God. At times even children were sacrificed to appease God, but this is unreasonable. It is not possible for man to attain God's level. And then suddenly there comes the Good News that a man is born who really can reach God, a man who can say of himself: "He who has seen me has seen the Father" (Jn. 14, 9). And he not only says this, but he proves it through his perfect and complete humanity, by being a man par excellence, by being both divine and human. It is he who shows us the way to come to God. He gives us the possibility of also becoming ideal men, who will not break the bruised reed, who can forgive and forget, who are in full communication with each other, for once one man has reached the divine, the way lies open to all men: "I am the way. . . . No one comes to the Father but through me" (Jn. 14, 6).

It is because of these ideas that on special occasions a solemn entrance of the priest is fitting, thus exemplifying the coming of Christ. On such occasions, however, we would ask that all other opening ceremonials be omitted except for the greeting of the priest to the people and a Collect-prayer, in which all the intentions of those present are gathered together.

The Confession of Faults

Upon other occasions more attention could be paid to the confession of faults as the beginning of the service. Everyone feels that it is really a distressing situation that Christians often fall short of the mark in love for neighbor, since religion without love of neighbor is impossible. Since the time of Marx it has been repeatedly stated—and often correctly—that Christians are deserters of the earth, that they pray for and speak about heaven so much that they forget the earth, that they only hold out the prospect of heaven to people who suffer need, while really doing very little to make this earthly life livable. The apostle James put his finger on this sore point when he said: "If a brother or sister is ill-clad and in lack of daily food, and one of you says to them, 'Go in peace, be warm, and filled,' without giving them the things needed for the body, what does it profit" (Jas. 2, 15-16). Christians, as well as the Church, are actually guilty before God and man. It is therefore right and very desirable that the liturgy give expression to this by a confession of faults on the part of the priest as well as of those present.

A new idea of the priesthood is emerging. If in the past he was a man with the "power to consecrate" and the "power to absolve," and often acted as the infallible conscience of men which determined the important and the trivial, and judged whether there were reasons to eat meat on Friday or miss Mass on Sunday, the priest is now coming closer to men, as the one who wishes to be of service, who, like the Lord, wants to be a fellowman par excellence. This leads to a different manner of preaching and speaking. It finds expression in his form of dress which is gradually becoming more like that of the other people. He is no longer "the reverend son" who walks between father and mother; his tendency is to walk on the left. Most priests have no desire of being put back on the pedestal from which they have descended. This does not lessen their priestly ideal, but it does give it a different aspect. Often the priest will discover how little he corresponds to the ideal of being of service to all. The confession of faults at the beginning of the service in which he leads the other faithful can only be salutary both to him and to them. A sincere confession of faults by the priest will make all aware that he, too, is a man, and that there really is no reason to be ashamed to manifest one's conscience to a priest. There is no human inclination toward evil which a priest does not know from his own experience.

There is yet another reason why the confession of faults at the beginning of the eucharistic service is desirable. When all is said and done, it remains true that God does not accept the gifts or hear the prayers of people who bear grudges against their brothers. "So if you are offering your gift at the altar, and there remember that your brother has something against you, leave your gift there before the altar and go; first be reconciled to your brother and then come and offer your gift" (Mt. 5, 23-24). This is plain talk. Furthermore, it answers a real human need. Every man has a vital need for purification. This can easily be shown. It is evident from the hundred and one ways in which we try to justify what was bad. It is also evident that this justifying does not purify. Real purification demands that we honestly acknowledge our faults and confess them to God. We know that in the sacrament of penance we are given this certitude of forgiveness; this sacrament is the only way of attaining purification when there is a total break with God or with his people, the Church. Apart from such a total break, which we call mortal sin, pardon can also be obtained outside the confessional. An honest and upright confession of faults before the beginning of the eucharist really effects forgiveness and purification.

Perhaps it will be helpful here to point to another aspect which is also possibly overlooked too much in the sacrament of penance: the effect of all our acts, and thus also of our sinful deeds, on our fellowmen. Between God and us there is our fellowman. There simply is no such a thing as making peace with God without making peace with man. We are fortunate that recent developments concerning the sacrament of penance are clarifying this aspect. We must also confess our faults to one another and grant pardon. The public confession of faults at the beginning of the eucharist does exactly this. It is precisely in the openness of this confession of fault, where everyone accuses himself of having missed the mark, that we can express the awareness that our sinful deeds have injured our fellowman and that we want to acknowledge our faults to them. Then, in the measure by which we forgive each other, we will also receive forgiveness from the Lord.

This gives the great principle of pardon enunciated in the Our Father: "Forgive us our trespasses as we forgive those who trespass against us."

The Prayer of Supplication

A student who had been taking it rather easy all year and then began a fervent novena nine days before his examinations, lighting a votive candle each day and attending Mass, was quite disappointed with God when he failed nonetheless. He was just as disappointed as the farmer who in the course of an extremely dry summer was faced by the choice of installing an irrigation system at great expense or of praying for rain. He chose the latter, which was less expensive. Notwithstanding, his crop was a failure. He also was disappointed with God. "Prayer doesn't help anymore either; everything is changing nowadays," he complained. It is true that in the Middle Ages processions of prayer and penance were held in order to obtain liberation from contagious diseases. Modern science gives the patient an injection. The results of the penitential processions was that the sickness continued to rage and possibly at times even increased because of the mutual contact. The result of injections is that the sickness often disappears.

This may give the impression that God really does not have much to do with the matter, that prayer produces little result, and that one should appeal to technology and science rather than to God. It would seem that the factory is more productive than the church, and the hospital more effective than a novena.

It is a fact that we progressively ask God for fewer and fewer favors. Nor is this so important anymore. The more we can accomplish by technology, the less we have to bother God. God is only necessary where and when our modern science fails. God has become a sort of reserve on our team. He is called upon to play when one of the regulars is missing. One is compelled to say that God is losing ground. In fact it is so; this strange God is losing ground. The question is: Is this truly God? God is not a reserve on our team. God is not a rival of technique and science. God is not a substitute for the factory. God is not a "trot" in an examination. A God who permits students who do not study to pass, or substitutes for an irrigation system, or removes contagious diseases independently from medical science does not exist; such a God is merely the product of our fantasy.

Who is God, then? In any event he is not something apart from us, apart from the world, apart from technology, apart from science. He is the ground-of-being of all these things; he is present and operative in them. Is there, then, no difference between God and the world? There is a difference. God exists, and he *must* exist. We exist, but we could have *not* existed. The world would not be much different without us. But without God the world would not be. Without God there would be no technology, no human science, no electricity. Yet this does not mean that God must sit down in a medical laboratory in order to discover a remedy for cancer because we are asking for one. God gave us faculties, and we must work with these faculties.

One may ask: "Does it make sense to pray, since in the long run we have to do it ourselves?" It all depends on what we mean by prayer. If prayer only means that we try to compel God to do our will, to supplement either our weakness or our laziness, then it really does not make sense to pray. But prayer is something else. It is an acknowledgment that without him we would not even exist. It is an acknowledgment that he is the creator; it is bowing our heads before the almighty. It is not God who must do our bidding; it is we who must fulfill God's will.

Prayer is to acknowledge that God is present in and also works through modern technology and science. Every prayer, to be good, must have this basic attitude: "God, let me know your will and fulfill it."

One must, therefore, advise a student not to choose between study and prayer, but to do both: to study and to pray. He must pray when there are difficulties, because it is then that he experiences most clearly that he is nothing and that God is almighty. When, because of duress, he feels his smallness, he is in a position to pray. But if he resorts to prayer instead of study, then he lowers God to the status of a "set of notes," which is an insult rather than an honor to him. God gave him his faculties; he must employ these gratefully. This is God's will; honest prayer will tell him as much. In like manner the farmer must not choose between installing an irrigation system or making a novena; he must do both. He will naturally do well by buying an irrigation system; God did not give such powers to nature in vain. He is not honored by substituting a cheap prayer for expensive equipment; God is simply not a substitute for an irrigation system.

Thus prayer is not to compel God to do our will. The essence of prayer is to acknowledge that God is master of all, to acknowledge his sovereignty.

Among the various rites of the eucharist there is a prayer of petition which expresses all this beautifully. This prayer of petition is just a remnant remaining from a longer litany. One may even suggest that this prayer might as well be omitted, now that the "bidding" prayers have been restored. To us, however, it does not seem out of place to have such a prayer of petition at the beginning of the service; however, let it be somewhat more articulate by allowing the whole community to participate. Occasionally one hears the remark that many are not particularly happy with the "Lord, have mercy on us" translation of the Kyrie Eleison. The prayer is very short and is not particularly suitable for an authentic acclamation, especially when there is not a preceding announcement of intention. Yet this short cry for help has a deep meaning. It addresses Christ with his title of honor, "Lord." This is all the more true in languages that use the same word in addressing fellowmen, whereas in English we use the word "sir." Then it is in danger of receiving the same connotation as the inscription of a letter, "Dear Sir," or of a formal address, "Sir." Originally this term signified supreme authority, one who was lord and master over the person and life of all his subjects. That is why strictly speaking only the man par excellence, Jesus Christ, is the Lord. Furthermore in the New Testament this word connotes the resurrection, for it is in and through his resurrection that Jesus Christ was exalted and made Lord.

When we say, "Have mercy on us," we place ourselves on the other side of his majestic sovereignty. There we stand in our own places, very small, very humble, very indigent, and we ask for compassion and mercy. This short prayer expresses the proper relationships well. It compares the highest with the lowest. In this short prayer of supplication the risen Lord and mortal man stand side by side.

This meaning comes to the fore especially when the prayer is sung. It then gives man a real opportunity to set forth his need. Then it becomes a real prayer for a man who knows no way out of his difficulties, for parents who are used and abused by their children who do not know or are forgetful what the former are doing for them. Then it can also become authentic prayer for young people, adolescents, who face life with anxiety because only a few seem to understand them. Then it can also become a prayer for lonely people and for others who feel God has abandoned them because their life does not correspond to God's wishes. In such a prayer God is nearer than one surmises. Jesus came precisely for the weak, the sinful, the spiritually destitute man. He seeks precisely those people for whom there is no other solution than the

Lord's overwhelming mercy and his boundless readiness to forgive.

He came not for the righteous but for sinners, for the simple reason that healthy people do not need a physician, but the sick do (Lk. 5, 31-32).

Looked at in this way, the prayer of supplication can indeed be one of the ways in which the solemnity may begin. Our concern is that too much that is different is used simultaneously in order to open the service. Too much can miss the mark, even with this exceptionally meaningful tradition.

The Collect

At the end of the opening ceremonial we have yet another prayer which merits our special respect and attention because of its historical background and its pointedness in thought and language.

Every man will occasionally come upon a period when he must admit that prayer is difficult if not impossible. There can be many reasons for this. It can be because of ordinary dryness or a too material disposition. It can also be a consequence of praying wrongly. It is certainly not an exception to find that some people, as far as their prayer is concerned, are still wearing the shoes of childhood without realizing how they pinch. As a man grows to maturity, he develops in all directions. He learns languages, technique and manners, but often gives little attention to the development of a mature spiritual life. This is especially the case in prayer. Thus it is advisable to take a few lessons in prayer from the school where it is taught best, the Church. Here we have a tradition of 2,000 years of experience in prayer.

This prayer does not begin with petitions, though such is our own inclination. It always begins with adoration of

God's majesty, praising his glory. Its purpose is not to put God in the proper mood, but to set the proper relationship. This is clearly seen in a chance example: "Almighty God, you restore innocence and you love innocence." This is a hymn of praise of God's holiness and of his love for innocence.

If in this prayer one has encountered God as the Innocent One who effects and loves innocence, then the ground has been laid for petition. Someone who is so entirely holy must be pleased when others ardently desire to live in the same innocence. Therefore this prayer dares to ask: "Turn our lives toward yourself, give us your Spirit, so that we may be strong in our faith and innocent in our actions."

The third element of this prayer is an appeal to Jesus Christ as the Son of God and our Lord. Realizing that our prayer cannot reach the endless majesty of God, we appeal to the most ideal and perfectly innocent man who is the apple of God's eye: "This we ask not of ourselves, but through Jesus Christ, your Son and our Lord." The final word of this prayer is the "Amen." When we ask a class of children what this Hebrew word means, there are always a few who immediately put up their hands as a sign of readiness for showing off their wisdom; they say that "Amen" means "It is finished." This childish error demands correction. "Amen" means that the prayer is approved, that we set our signature to it, that it is stamped with our seal, that all those present are wholly in agreement.

The name of this prayer is the Collect. As the term already indicates, it has the nature of gathering together. In other words, something has to precede this prayer; there must be an invitation to prayer and a period of silence for prayer. The shortest form of this invitation is: "Let us pray." Perhaps it would be well from time to time to expand this invitation. Thus one might say: "Let us pray for a few moments for what concerns us most." We have examples of this in the Holy Week liturgy. There the participants are asked to pray for prisoners, for catechumens, for widows and orphans, and for seafarers. Such an invitation to prayer, followed by a period of silence, can also have its place outside of Holy Week. In our opinion the periods of silence for prayer are much too formal in many churches because they consist of only a few seconds. Often they merely give the impression that the priest cannot readily find the right place in his book rather than of being an exhortation that they should apply themselves to silent prayer. If this silence is to be a meaningful and fruitful silence, then two things are necessary: first, an invitation to prayer; second, sufficient time. It is thus of prime importance that, in the renewal of the liturgy, room is made for periods, even longer periods, of quiet. There is the tendency to make our liturgy a "talking" liturgy. This cheats the individual person; this is the occasion for much complaint. These complaints are honest and justified. They come from people who can no longer talk and who have little inclination to have the quiet for prayer allotted in seconds. When so many people are gathered together, it is well to remember that each one of them leads his own life with his own difficulties and his own concerns. There may be some among them who are celebrating a birthday and there may be others who have just lost a dear one. Each one has something to say to God in his own way, and each one has a right to this period. He must therefore also have an opportunity to pray.

It is only when the period of silence has been filled in this manner that the Collect acquires its proper place as the opening prayer for the whole service. This prayer can be combined with one of the other possibilities mentioned above for opening the service. We hope that the renewal of the opening rite will, in any event, not be delayed long, and that this renewal will make the beginning of the service somewhat more meaningful than is now the case.

CHAPTER THREE

The Service of the Word

Symbols

By our words we share ourselves with others. God also used the Word to share himself with us. Here we are touching upon something profoundly human. Whenever people want to establish contact with each other, they use a material means which they inspire with life. This is something very wonderful and of great importance. Before we analyze the word as such, it will be helpful to consider symbols in general. This is all the more true when people consider symbols unreal; and people do, as is obvious from the remark: "This is only the symbol."

It is true that the face is the mirror of the soul. We can often read a man's character and temperament in his face. In any event there are many emotions which manifest themselves on the face: love, hatred, contempt, illusion, gratitude, sympathy—in short, the whole inner man can be seen on his face.

There is something uncanny about this. The whole face of the man can be described as a component of blood vessels, nerves, tissues, eyes, hair. Yet love or disdain cannot be expressed as any one of these. The spiritual aspect of the face is something intangible, but it is there nonetheless. With a friendly, lovely mien we share our love with others. How many love songs ask for only a smile?

Man's life is filled with symbols which are beacons,

messengers of something spiritual. A country's flag is more than nylon or linen; it contains a spiritual element which we have incorporated into it in one way or another. This component cannot be detached by a microscope, but everyone feels that it is something real. Whoever rips a flag or soils it or steps on it desecrates a part of our country; he offends our deepest feelings. Looked at naturally, such a flag is only a piece of nylon or linen, but we animate this material thing with a spirit.

In like manner a wedding ring is more than a circular band of gold. Such a ring actually imbeds one's fidelity, as is obvious when one angrily strips the ring from his finger and throws it on the ground. Such a person throws down more than a little band of gold; he throws away his troth.

When Pope Paul gave a chalice to Patriarch Athenagoras, he gave him more than a chalice; he offered his brotherhood in this sacrament of unity. When the two embraced each other, they did more than merely place their arms around each other's shoulders; they filled this ceremonial with warmth, something purely spiritual. They animated this material posture.

In like manner we use symbols to express ourselves when we stand in God's presence—that is, we animate certain material postures and thus express exteriorly what we experience interiorly. We commune with God through these symbols.

Whoever wants to show reverence to God genuflects. Whoever wants to manifest his sorrow to God strikes his breast. Whoever wants to show his trust in God folds his hands. To fold one's hands is really to compress them so as to be totally recollected and express one's complete concentration on God. Whoever wants to consecrate himself to God makes the sign of the cross. To kneel means to make oneself small so that it can be seen that we regard ourselves as much less than God, that we acknowledge his greatness.

Why do we strike our breasts? When in our daily lives we commit a stupid mistake, we automatically tend to acknowledge this immediately. We clench our hands against our head as if to say: "How could I be so dumb?" When we have committed a fault against God, we should really crush our sinful heart. We want to stand before him with a crushed heart; therefore, we strike our breasts. That is why we do this also when we say "through my fault," or "Lord, I am not worthy," or "Lord, be merciful to me, a sinner." The action is appropriate. It would be unintelligible were it to accompany the words "Holy, holy, holy." It would then mean something like: "How holy I am."

It is customary to stand at the Gospel. This is to manifest our readiness to accomplish the message. We would also suggest that people remain seated during the service of the Word, even at the reading of the Gospel, to indicate an attitude of quiet and willingness to listen. The change from one position to another is disturbing to many people, and it does not foster the atmosphere of recollection which is necessary for careful listening.

What we have said about all these postures is also applicable to the words we speak. No human word is a mere movement of the air. No boy or girl in love would be very happy if their sweetheart were to give them a tape upon which there would only be the repetition of the phrase "I love you." These mechanized words would indeed be merely a movement of the air. A word is alive only when it is spoken by a living person.

Of course, natural science demonstrates how sound is generated by the movement of the air. One can almost see how the strings of a big bass viol whip the air and generate the somber tone. When people utter sound by singing or speaking, one cannot see the vocal cords but it is evident that they move the air. The movement of the mouth and the tongue gives these sounds certain nuances, and thus we speak. But is speaking merely a moving of the air? In this case it is really a remarkable movement. Experience shows that by speaking we can make others blissfully happy or despairingly sad. We observe that scolding hurts, that praise elates. There is no other sound-producing instrument which can cause similar effects. Naturally the neighbors can become quite disturbed when one of the children in the neighborhood is learning how to play his trumpet and has not yet accomplished the art, but this is something entirely different from being addressed disparagingly. What is it in this movement of sound which can make a person so happy or so discouraged?

In speech we encounter the same intangible element as in the usage of symbols. We are endowed with a sort of creative power. We are capable of changing the value of material things, to give them life, to animate them. We can pledge our troth with a ring, our respect with a genuflection, the love of our country with a flag. In like manner we are able to put life into the inanimate movement of air; this is the marvel of speaking. We are empowered to express our thoughts and emotions in words. A word is filled with our own personal being. It is filled with our spiritual wealth—or destitution! When a man speaks, he shares his thoughts with others. In the spoken word the other really encounters the feeling of the speaker. His spirit is present in the movement of the air.

The other party is capable of accepting the word. It does not remain outside him; it penetrates deep within him, to the very depth of his soul. Two spiritual beings, two people, then come in contact with each other. Such at least is the case if the other person opens himself, if he makes room within himself for the spirit of the speaker.

It is superfluous to spend much time proving that words really are capable of making another person happy. Every one of us has discovered this by personal experience; a hearty word never misses its mark. In like manner a hateful word never misses its mark either. How much and how great sadness has been occasioned by the misuse of words!

Words live; they are alive. The thoughts and emotions of the speaker are embodied in his words. A word is filled with a man's spiritual treasure. Words share this store with others. In a certain sense it is true to say that the speaker gives up the monopoly to his innermost being by sharing it with others.

It is obvious that speaking bears a close relationship with loving. The essence of love is to give oneself to another. To speak is to do the same; by speaking one shares one's spiritual wealth with another. Word and love are thus closely allied. Thus St. John can say, "God is love," but he also says, and must say, "The Word [is] God" (Jn. 1, 1).

Even when we address our words to God—and this we call "prayer"—we pledge our hearts and our minds. If the words of our prayers are not filled with our inner life, then they are merely a lifeless movement of the air, as inanimate as the buzz of a machine. Such prayer is rightfully rejected and detested in scripture: "This people honors me with their lips, but their heart is far from me" (Mt. 15, 8). Everyone senses how offensive and belittling it is to address someone thoughtlessly; in such a case there is no question of human communication. Speaking to God in this manner is no more fitting. Here, too, our speaking must be filled with our thoughts and our feelings, with our interior wealth or our interior destitution, if it is going to be authentic prayer. It is for this reason that it is so necessary that the vernacular obtain a place in the liturgy.

God's Presence in the Word

God loves men. He who is infinitely happy wants to make others happy. This is his great and divine desire. And everything is of use to him in accomplishing this desire, even our human speech. That is why God spoke to men. He has filled our human sounds and signs with his thoughts and with the emotions of his sacred heart. God is truly present in his Word, because the Holy Spirit lives in his words.

If one is convinced that this Word is filled with God's Spirit, then it is also obvious that the Word of God has unimaginable power. Isaiah says that God's Word does not return empty but accomplishes what it was sent to do (Is. 55, 11). That this is true can readily be seen from the story of creation. God sent forth his Word and it accomplished what it was commissioned to do. Everything was made by his Word, and without him nothing was made that is (Jn. 1). The world was dead, but God spoke and it was filled with life. The water was calm, but God spoke and it stirred with fish. God spoke, and God saw that it was good (Gen. 1). That God's Word is endowed with great power is evident also from the effect that Jesus' Word has upon men. A single word spoken by him is capable of healing the servant of an officer. The man believed, and therefore he could say: "Lord, speak but the word and my servant will be healed" (Mt. 8, 8). A single word of his is capable of calling the apostles, of inviting an adulterous woman to reconsideration, and of turning a sinner into a saint. It would naturally be foolish to think that the Word had lost its power in our age. The Word is still capable of moving men in our day to overcome the greatest difficulties, to encourage them beyond measure, and to reveal God's will to each. If human words are capable of setting us on fire, just imagine what God's Word can do!

If this Word does in fact exercise comparatively little influence, the reason for this can not be in the Word itself but on our failure to be open to the Word. The Word is the vehicle and the instrument of the Spirit only when we make room for it. The fact is that reverence for God's

Word is growing; the fact is also that this reverence still leaves much to be desired. It is noteworthy how shocked one is whenever a priest accidentally drops a sacred host when distributing communion. And yet there is hardly any reaction whatever when, during the liturgy of the Word, God's Word goes unnoticed because no one is listening or because it is poorly read. There must be greater appreciation that God is present not only in heaven or in the host but also in his Word. For this reason great attention must also be given to the manner in which it is read.

God's Word also possesses the power of forgiveness. The priest expresses his faith in this power when, after the reading of the Gospel, he says: "May our sins be removed by the words of this Gospel." In the Divine Office the reading from the scripture is introduced by the words: "May the reading of the Gospel bring us support and salvation."

It seems therefore meaningful to us that in our churches the book of God's Word should be exposed prominently on a beautiful lectern, surrounded with flowers, and readily accessible to any chance visitor.

God's Words Are Heralds

God spoke the first word; he began. Thus man's word to God can only be an answer. This is apparent in the liturgy where we try to vivify our relationship with God in as meaningful a manner as possible. In the liturgy there are two movements, one from God to us and the other from us to God. God speaks, man answers; God redeems, man gives thanks; God reveals, man discovers and adores.

The liturgy is a huge mirror which catches God's light and reflects it again to him. This is very much the case in the eucharist. Here God's redemption overshadows man, and man becomes a participant in the redemption; man then in turn sends thanksgiving back to God. This same exchange also prevails in the liturgy of the Word: God addresses man, he reveals his love and exposes his plan; man's answer is a believing acceptance, a profession of faith.

In the proclamation of the Good News of salvation in the Epistle and the Gospel, we have the descending movement from God to man. We have already seen that there is a real descent. We are not dealing merely with images; the Word is more than sound. It is typical that in the holy scriptures the Word is regarded as something living, as a person, a herald, a messenger. Thus Isaiah writes: "The Lord has sent a word against Jacob, and it will light upon Israel" (Is. 9, 7). A word is not finished once it has been spoken: it continues to possess power; it remains alive and operative; it does something. It is no wonder then that Esau was so keenly upset when his twin brother Jacob had received the blessing from his aged father. It could not be recalled, it could not be undone. There was really nothing to do about it. His brother had received the blessing; he would be blessed with the fat of the earth and the abundance of grain and wine (Gen. 27, 28).

This is all the more the case with a written word. Pilate could not undo what he had determined: "What I have written, I have written" (Jn. 19, 22).

All this is especially applicable to the Word of God in the sacred scriptures. Here the Word is not merely a sound. It is a living substance; it does something. Thus God can say of his obstinate people: "I have slain them by the words of my mouth" (Hos. 6, 5). And he makes Jeremiah say: "Is not my word like fire, says the Lord, like a hammer which breaks the rock in pieces?" (Jer. 23, 29). In reference to the Messiah Isaiah says: "He shall smite the earth with the rod of his mouth, and with the breath of his lips he shall slay the wicked" (Is. 11, 4). Later on

Paul will avow that Christ will destroy the antichrist by the breath of his mouth (2 Thess. 2, 8).

The same must be said of the Epistle and the Gospel. These words may admittedly be invisible but they are real beings. They do something; they accomplish something. These words can effect our salvation, on the condition that man make room within himself for God's Spirit, which is brought to him by the Word.

When in the Gospel it is said: "The Father loves you" (Jn. 16, 27), this is not merely an affirmation: at the same moment the Father really loves us. When it is said: "Blessed are the poor in spirit" (Mt. 5, 3), then this has its effect at the very same moment. When it is said: "See that you do not despise one of these little ones; for I tell you that in heaven their angels always behold the face of my Father who is in heaven" (Mt. 18, 10), these words do something. When it is said: "Your sins are forgiven you. . . ." (Mt. 9, 2) or "Come to me all you who labor and are heavy laden, and I will give you rest" (Mt. 11, 28) or "Whoever believes in me shall never die" (Jn. 11, 26), then these words are heralds, messengers sent by God which accomplish what they have been commissioned to do.

Man's first response to these heralds must be faith. Thus God's proclamation of salvation is reflected, so to speak, in a large powerful mirror. This profession of faith may not be a mere mouthing of an empty formula, but it must be a convincing witness with the authentic nature of a response.

The whole proclamation of the Word has as its goal an invitation to faith, to arouse us to the obedience of faith, so that we may enter the liturgy of the sacrament with a living faith. This is the proper function of this service of the Word and the bible-reading in the liturgy. This is also the reason why the Church has kept all-night bible vigils. This is the reason why today the Church wants us to read the bible, to hold bible vigils. (Only then can the sacramental celebration of redemption become fruitful.) The liturgy of the Word is a brief form of bible service. No wonder, then, that Vatican Council II recommended that to fulfill our Sunday obligation we attend both services. This is an entirely different admonition than the one given formerly —when it was emphasized that the grave obligation of being present began only with the Offertory. Whoever was not present then had not fulfilled his Sunday obligation. Mortal sin entered with the Offertory! It is therefore also incorrect to speak about "the Foremass" as if this part were merely a preparation for the Mass proper.

It should be noticed here how the service of the Word forms part of all the sacraments. The ancient catechumenate was really nothing more than a prolonged service of the Word. This is equally true of the catechesis which is given the children in instruction in school, or which a father or a mother gives to their child when they speak of Christ. The most meaningful, the only really meaningful conclusion of such catechesis, whether in the school or in the home, is that it be followed by the celebration of the sacrament. Then only has the catechesis reached its proper goal. Whoever misses the liturgy of the Word misses the full content of the Lord's coming, of the salvation he brings in the eucharist.

The Homily

Many a person would breathe a sigh of relief if unexpectedly the homily were omitted from the eucharistic celebration. When conversation is dull, it can be livened by switching the topic to sermons. It is an undeniable fact that in many churches heads look up at the beginning of the homily to see whose turn it is to preach and then sink back with the expression: "Oh, it's him again."

Many reasons can be given for this attitude toward the

homily among many people. The diction is poor. The content is meager. There is a standing joke about the pastor who began his sermon by saying, "Dear parishioners, may I ask your special attention. I cannot preach today because I have something to say to you."

The fact remains that many have lost sight of the relationship between the homily and the eucharist. Unfortunately there has been and still exists the practice in some churches that during the sermon the celebrant goes to the sacristy in order to escape having to listen to the sermon. This practice has had a dour influence. It showed plainly that the sermon was something additional, that it did not have an essential tie-in with the whole celebration. Thank God, such practices belong mostly in the past.

Naturally there are a whole raft of excuses why the sermon is often of low caliber. Not every priest has the gift of speaking well; nonetheless, because of his mission he must proclaim the Word. Then there may be circumstances when he must preach as though nothing had happened when actually he has received some disturbing message shortly before the sermon. It can also happen that he must proclaim the Word while he himself is experiencing a deep crisis in his spiritual life. Furthermore, it burdens a preacher when some of his listeners keep on demanding that the sermon be very short, so short in fact that he really does not get a chance to touch on the subject he would like to speak about.

It should be noted emphatically here that the homily belongs to the eucharistic celebration and cannot be omitted. The Word of God is read, but the Word must become an actual message. It must be a meaningful message here and now to the people who are present. That is the purpose of the homily. This is nothing new; Christ had previously done it. When on a Sabbath morning he had read a piece from the scriptures in which it said: "The Spirit of the Lord shall come upon you," he set aside the scroll and began to make this message of God an actual one by his homily: "Today this scripture has been fulfilled in your hearing" (Lk. 4, 16-21; Jn. 18, 20). St. Paul followed a similar practice and proclaimed his message after the reading of the sacred scriptures.

It is not sufficient to set the bread of the Word before the reader; the bread must be broken for him. Just as the eucharistic celebration demands communion, so the bible reading demands the homily.

When we assert that priests are obligated to give great care to the homily, we must add immediately that the preacher as well as the listeners must be pervaded with great faith. Christ himself said of those who proclaim God's Word: "Who hears you, hears me" (Lk. 10, 16). Whoever would listen to a homily fruitfully must, so to speak, see the Lord standing behind the preacher, pointing to him and saying: "Whoever listens to him, listens to me." And then it really makes no difference whether the priest has a beautiful voice or not, whether he is an accomplished speaker or not, for one can then hear God's voice in him.

Fortified by such faith it actually becomes possible to listen fruitfully. Even the most learned theologian can listen beneficially to a sermon when assisted by this faith. He, too, will receive some instruction from this simple talk because it is the actualization of God's message.

Just as a mother senses herself borne along by the spirit of God when she tells her child about Jesus, because she is then the instrument by which God is bringing this child into contact with salvation, so the preacher is God's instrument for putting his listeners in contact with salvation.

Thus faith is necessary for both the hearers and the preacher. With faith there must also be prayer. The criticism of the sermon would be much more effective if it were accompanied by a prayer for the preacher. Even St. Paul would approve of this; he himself prayed that God would open the door of his mouth (Col. 4, 3). We can hardly imagine this for Paul, the preacher par excellence. Did he really experience difficulty in opening his mouth? We would rather say to him: "But Paul, it seems so easy for you!" Instead, Paul shakes his head and asks God to open the door of his mouth. Perhaps we would then like to say to him: "Really now, Paul! The important point is that people listen to you; you must pray for them, not for yourself. You know what you have to say to them." Paul would undoubtedly answer: "No, I must myself be aglow; I must myself be on fire." This must also be the prayer of those who are obliged to proclaim the Word.

The Response

There is a great difference in being present and in being attentive, as every teacher will be quick to agree. Hasn't every teacher often been annoyed because his pupils are not attentive? They are sitting in the class, they are present, but they are not listening.

This same difference between presence and participation can also be observed on the train, on the street corner, or any place where people are gathered in a group. Take the case of hundreds of people living together in a tenement house. These people live alongside each other, but they also live apart from each other. A person may feel absolutely alone in a large city, because people are not present to each other. In planes and elsewhere people regularly sit alongside each other. At times one can find them packed twenty or more in a place, standing next to each other, but they are not present to each other. They do not exist for each other. Only those people who exist for each other, who have spiritual contact with each other, are present-for-each-other. Then word is met by answer and address by response. Then one may speak of authentic presence.

In times past the expression "to attend Mass" was common. It is now used less frequently because everyone senses that it does not suffice. It refers only to presence; it says nothing about participation. Where the Mass is only "attended" there is no exchange of words, there is no dialogue, there is no speech. The Mass had actually become a purely clerical affair where only the priest was important. This evil is still far from being overcome. The size and structure of many a church make it particularly difficult to find a proper solution. Often there is a sizable separation between sanctuary and nave, accented occasionally by a barrier. The dimensions of some churches are so great, their seating capacity so large, that half of the occupants have hardly any sense of participation in what is going on. All this is much more possible in smaller structures. It is therefore puzzling why such enormous churches continue to be built and why on weekdays especially the eucharist is not celebrated in a more confined area. We are thinking of bedridden patients who would be overjoyed if they could participate in the eucharist right in their own room. We are thinking of the aged who can no longer leave their home, of the home visit in the evening which could be terminated with the celebration of the eucharist, of a get-acquainted evening for new parishioners either in the rectory or some other convenient room. The picture called forth by our large churches on a cold, wintry weekday with tens of thousands of empty seats in chilly, poorly illuminated buildings is hardly inviting. On days like that we would rather have a well-prepared, simple house-liturgy. It is obvious, of course, that this would demand a simplified form of the eucharistic celebration, with simplified rites. Undoubtedly the participants would quickly get the idea that the eucharist is something in which they are closely associated.

It is well known that there was a period in which the entire participation of the people consisted in looking at the sacred host at the Consecration. Even the sick and the aged were dragged into Church for that moment, because many fostered the superstition that they would see the sacred host before they died. There was no thought of active participation. Fortunately, this time has now passed.

God is truly present in his Word. He speaks to us personally. Our listening must not be done passively. It must mean active attention to his proposal. Whoever is present in this way will unquestionably feel the compulsion to respond. This response of faith shall be a "yes" of commitment to the message contained in the readings.

As a matter of fact this "yes" is put in words by the saying of the creed. Yet it must be noted that the printed text does not constitute a profession of faith. It becomes this only when it is pronounced, when these words are filled with the spirit of those present. Symbols come into being only when they are animated by our thoughts and emotions. Christmas cards with a cold and formal printing of the sender's name can hardly be considered symbols. This is all the more true of the symbol of our faith, the creed.

This creed expressed the faith of the apostles, especially when they gave their lives for it. It expressed the faith of the martyrs, especially when they were being put to death for it. It expresses the faith of the Church when the faithful order their lives according to its principles. Then one can speak of participation, of response to the Word of God.

Different Ways of Participation

Complaints are made that the renewal of the liturgy has practically discarded the usage of the popular missal. It is our opinion that the use of the daily missal as it was encouraged by the liturgical movement in the beginning of this century did much good, but that it really was an intermediate step toward further development. Until recently this effort to place a missal in the hands of the faithful had great significance. There was little opportunity for active participation; thus it was an enormous step in the right direction to have recourse to the missal, so that those present could be able at least to follow what the priest was saying and doing. But now circumstances have changed for the better. Opportunity is now given for active participation instead of merely reading along from the missal. Furthermore, there is a growing understanding that those present have a very special function at the service.

This aspect was hardly fostered by the daily missals. In fact the missal was scarcely more than a small edition of the altar missal. The latter is a book which actually is a combination of several books. It may be compared with a musical score in which all the parts are registered. Thus we have the part of the choir, of the lector, of the reader, of the faithful, and of the deacon—in short, all these parts are published under one cover. Anyone acquainted with the activity of a symphony orchestra knows that no player uses the full score to follow his part. Only the conductor has such a score lying before him. It requires a particular skill to read such a score. Each player has his own part, which suffices for him and which is much easier to read. Furthermore, many missals are not clear in determining who takes what part. The division of activity which really ought to be very clear in every eucharistic celebration is actually not mentioned. In addition, there is the difficulty that the eucharistic celebration as it is performed in many places leaves the firm impression of being exclusively the affair of the priest.

There is not much purpose in speaking about the historical background of this situation. The fact is that in the course of the centuries practically all the parts were taken over by one person—the priest. Notwithstanding this, the truth is that all must take part in the celebration, each in his own manner, with his own function and with his own duty. In other words, there are different ways of participation. The priest as priest, in his position as leader, must preside in his proper place. The singers will exercise a different form of participation precisely because of what they are doing. The acolytes, the sacristan, the deacons—all have their own places, their own manner of participation. There is a definite division of roles. This is necessary if the communal character of the celebration is to be fully expressed.

First, there is the role of the priest who presides. One cannot avoid the impression that his function as president is not exercised properly because he still performs many functions that really do not belong to him. Here we are thinking of the reading of texts which should only be sung by the schola—for example, the Introit, the Gradual, the Offertory and the Communion Hymn. Hence we might ask ourselves just how far can one go in saying it is reasonable that these texts should be merely read. There is definitely something out of place when in a low Mass, after the distribution of holy communion, the priest reads: "The sparrows have their nests. . . ." This kind of thing is strange in our daily lives. No one of us would think of merely reciting or saying "Happy Birthday to you" on someone's birthday. This has to be sung; if not, it should be omitted entirely. Similarly, the alternating of the Kyrie between the priest and the faithful can hardly be considered the proper role of the president. It seems equally improper to alternate it between the choir, or the cantor, and the other faithful. The same is true for the Gloria. The Collect, on the contrary, is a typically priestly prayer. The readings, especially of the Epistle, should be entrusted to a separate lector. The preparation of the chalice and also the purification of the chalice at the end of the service is obviously the role of one of the servers. In thus clarifying the function of the priest, his proper role will be seen more clearly to consist in the pronunciation of the great eucharistic prayer.

With the role of the president we have mentioned that of the lector; this is generally passed over rapidly. If the vernacular is going to be used throughout the whole Mass, especially in the eucharistic prayer, then the need for a separate lector for the scriptural readings, especially for those of the Epistle, becomes all the more urgent. Without such a lector, the priest would be reading all the time during the service. Even a change of voices thus becomes most welcome. Yet apart from this, as has already been noted, it is necessary to divide the functions in order to express the communal character of the celebration more clearly.

Still another manner of participation is that of the acolytes. That preference is given to adult acolytes is obvious. But then care must be taken that these adult persons also be given an adult's task, and that they perform adult actions, with adult instruments. The small water and wine cruets with the miniature handkerchief, preferably folded into nine parts, had best be relegated to the past.

The first chapter has already commented on the task of the others who are present—that is, their active participation in the liturgy. It is a participation in the service to the Lord. They should especially have a profound understanding that during the celebration of the eucharist they are present at the banquet of the Lord. Then the conclusion would obviously follow that their participation will find its deepest expression in a loving eating of that sacred bread in a spirit of thanksgiving and praise.

When God's Word is proclaimed, it is the duty of those present to listen with faith and to make an honest effort to apply this Word to their personal lives. This requires reflection. For the time being a longer period for reflection is wanting in our liturgy; opportunity for such reflection is sought during the Offertory.

The Canon, with which we still have to deal, is really an extended table prayer uttered by the priest wherein all thanks and praises are offered to God. There is then no need for a lengthy demonstration that it is the corresponding task of the faithful to associate themselves spiritually and wholeheartedly with this thanksgiving, which will then be expressed enthusiastically in the singing of the Sanctus. This is a song which belongs to all those present, and is thus not the domain of either the schola or the choir. The same is true of the Our Father, and especially of the "great Amen" at the end of the table prayers. It has even been said that this "great Amen" is the most important word uttered by the faithful during the entire eucharistic period. This is obvious if we compare it with the acclamation that is given the eulogy on the occasion of some celebration or jubilee. There one expresses his approval by applauding, by singing a proposed song, or by drinking a toast. Here the approval is manifested by the "Amen," which means nothing more than wholehearted assent.

Whoever is not merely present at the eucharist but participates in the fullest sense feels a compulsion to express this participation. We shall never succeed in realizing the full intent of Christ—a love-inspired fellowship gathered around his table—unless everyone takes part in this dialogue and is unhampered by considerations of human respect. Human respect does play a large role in our lives. It can sustain our effort, but it can also be a dreadful hindrance. It is generally a hindrance at our Sunday meetings. Many do not feel free to be spontaneous because they are afraid of what others might think. Such people will sing or pray with a loud voice only if all the others do so. But because not everyone does so, they do not either. And thus things keep on rotating in a vicious circle!

Word and Eucharist

Even if a person is hardly aware of God's existence, God loves him nonetheless. The case is similar to that of a small child who is constantly loved by his parents even when it is not able to reciprocate. It is God's love which gives man existence; it is also his love which keeps him in existence. If God were to cease loving us for a moment we would immediately cease to exist. God loved us first; every loving act of man can only be a response.

When we love other people, we do so because we find something sympathetic, something attractive in them. Our love does not make someone sympathetic; it is drawn by the attractive element in another. When God loves men he is not drawn by us; he does not love man because man is lovable. When God loves us, he makes us lovable. His love is creative. His love effects goodness. When we respond to God's love, that love is created and called forth by God. This is also the case when Christians assemble to celebrate the liturgy. It is God who calls us to the liturgy, to the worship of God and the service of man; it is he who makes this possible.

The liturgy of the Word has the Epistle and the Gospel as its central point. They are read from the book that has God as its author. Here man hears what God thinks of him, how he loves him, what he has done for him, what he is planning for him, what he expects in our attitudes toward God and man. In the Gospel Christ is quite clearly represented as the servant of men. He is depicted as the one who did not come to be served, but to give his life in the service of others.

All this points the way to true liturgy, to a correct attitude toward God and man: "A new commandment I give to you, that you love one another. . . ." (Jn. 13, 34); "By this all men will know that you are my disciples, if you love one another. . . ." (Jn. 13, 35); "As you did it to one of the least of these my brethren, you did to me" (Mt. 25, 40).

This liturgy of the Word comprises the foremost part of the Mass. It is read by the lector, its praises are sung by the choir, it is explained in the homily, and accepted in faith by the entire congregation. This Word teaches what liturgy is.

After the liturgy of the Word, the Lord invites us to the liturgy of the sacrificial meal. This liturgy has as its centerpiece a table, which is also an altar. As before, liturgy here also consists in worship of God and service to man. The Preface and Canon form an extended table prayer of praise and thanksgiving to God who created the world. He is the creator of color and sound, of flower and leaf. He is the one who conceived and brought into being the creature who is man. He is the one who revealed the depth and the beauty of his mercy in his Son, who lived and died for us and thus conquered death. The Son atoned for sin and thus rendered powerless its consequence, death. He is also the one who makes it possible for us to re-create in mutual love this world into a new world of peace and love. In this table prayer we give God thanks through his Son who is present among us and offers himself again under these sacramental signs.

Following this hymn of praise and thanksgiving the Lord offers us his love in the token of food and drink. It is then up to us to associate ourselves in this solemn act of gratitude to God by eating and drinking, by giving our consent to the loving invitation to make a covenant of confidence with God. In the face of such great love of God toward man, one cannot remain a curious bystander. God's supreme gift of himself arouses a response in us.

Here we can only say with Christ: "Look, Father! Here I am to do your will." This will of the Father, so perfectly exemplified by his Son, is the source of man's salvation and happiness. We are moved with desire to accomplish this will of the Father.

The result of all this is that the Christian becomes more a man. He becomes man as God became man—that is, he will make every effort to share and to alleviate the sorrow, the distress, the suffering, the hunger, the solitude of his fellowman. Thus the liturgy within the church demands a liturgy outside the church. The worship of God postulates availability toward man. Worship becomes humanitarian. Liturgy and life are identified.

CHAPTER FOUR

The Covenant

The Covenant as a Guarantee of Security

Someone once asked an ordinary group of young people the question: "What does it mean to you that God made a covenant with us?" The answer was surprisingly uniform: "Nothing!" One would have liked to have had a different answer—something not as terribly disappointing as that indifferent and cold "Nothing!"

This answer is inexplicable. Every week, at least fifty-two times a year, every Catholic stands face to face with that covenant. In every Mass resound the words of the Lord: "This is my blood of a new and eternal covenant that has been shed for you unto the remission of sins." In spite of this weekly commemoration, this weekly encounter with the very heart of our worship, there was the answer: "It means nothing to us!" We are tempted to say: "Poor Church! She seems to live in the illusion that we want to celebrate this covenant, to regard it as a feast, as a solution for our situation. How naive! The Church is mistaken! For most people the Mass is far from being a feast; it is rather an annoying obligation."

It may perhaps appear somewhat profane to borrow the language of insurance policies when speaking of the covenant between God and man. This can admittedly give rise to an entirely erroneous belief, leaving the impression that faith is some sort of an insurance company for eternal life, with the twelve articles of the Apostles' Creed as the policy, and good works as the premium.

Yet the covenant between God and man does give an assurance about which we must say a few words. It is precisely this aspect that must have some appeal to us of this century, because we feel so insecure and are constantly seeking for security. The modern man attempts to establish his security on all sides. Our streets are marked with striped crossings, there are stoplights at the corners, there are warnings to prevent accidents, there are seat belts, and so on. We want to reduce risks to a minimum. No time has ever been so fearful as our own.

How often young people are undecided when it comes to choosing a state of life! Is this girl, is this young man, going to be mine for good? Should I take that risk? In seminaries and monasteries young people experience similar crises when they must make their definitive decision. The decline in vocations is attributed to a growing fear of binding oneself for life. More and more one hears it said that man is even incapable of doing this.

Our age demands security because we are so insecure. Thus it is really no surprise when contemporary people say: "That God made a covenant with us tells us nothing." Yet it is precisely this covenant that gives us the security of faith that God is well disposed to us, that God forgives us our sins, that everything between us is in order, that we need never despair because the blood of the covenant is the blood of Christ shed for the remission of our sins. What does this mean?

The history of salvation as it is described in the bible gives an answer. When we make a pact in our daily affairs, we do this in order to obtain a firm footing. We want to put an end to conditions of fear and uncertainty. Thus we can imagine that the childless Abraham felt insecure when God bade him to go to a strange land. He was no longer a young man; his wife was old, and she had remained childless. The land which was promised him had yet to be conquered. What could two people do? Were they to mount a chariot, to seize bow and arrow, lance and shield, and take to the field against a superior power of young, vital troops armed to the teeth? Abraham felt the earth sinking away beneath his feet. He felt insecure and frightened. He wanted to end this situation; therefore, he asked Yahweh for a sign, and Yahweh answered with the covenant. This established our security. Yahweh's covenant is something so strong, so inviolable, that when Yahweh makes a covenant with someone there is no longer room for doubt or insecurity.

Alliances are also decisive in times of political crisis. In the conquest of the Holy Land one fortified city after another fell into the hands of the Jews. The Gibeonites saw themselves threatened; not a single city had been able to withstand the onslaught of Joshua. Now their turn had come; the army of Israel would soon be at their city gates. Panic prevailed; nervously they deliberated the situation. They knew that Joshua did not want to make a covenant with the inhabitants of the country. Therefore they devised a ruse: they disguised themselves as people from a distant country and asked for a covenant. Joshua did not detect their deception and actually made an alliance with them in the conviction that they were people from a distant land. When later he discovered they were inhabitants of a city that he was on the verge of conquering, there was nothing more to do about it. When he found that he had made a covenant with these people, he was helpless. He could not undo a covenant, for whoever would break a covenant would call God's wrath upon himself. Notwithstanding the dissatisfaction of his soldiers and of his people, Joshua was forced to leave this city of the Gibeonites undisturbed. The covenant had been made and there was no way to annul it (Jos. 9, 1-15).

This is the biblical view of a covenant: inviolable,

strong, holy, firm. It establishes absolute, unquestionable security. Doubt is excluded. This is the way the bible invites us to have a proper appreciation of God's covenant. When in the eucharist a covenant is established—a covenant giving us assurance that our sins are forgiven, that God loves us, that God wishes us well—then doubt is no longer possible. God wants to make us happy. This is guaranteed by the covenant.

Saved by Love through the Covenant

Since Yahweh had made a covenant with his people on Sinai, the pious Israelite knew that he was safe with God. This was not some mere pious imagery but actual reality. Yahweh himself had said that at his altar a man could find protection and security (Exod. 21, 14), and it actually happened more than once that people, who were being sought to be put to death, fled to the sanctuary and there seized hold of the horns of the altar. No one would dare to lay hands on even his most hated enemy there. He had sought and found his refuge with Yahweh. No wonder then that the pious man prayed: "I will dwell in the house of the Lord all the days of my life" (Ps. 23, 6). That was the sacred, inviolable right of asylum. Woe to him who violated this right!

There are many to whom it seemingly means nothing that God made a covenant with man. This is remarkable! When a child is troubled, it seeks its mother and clings to her. During the war the people in war-torn countries huddled together in damp cellars. A fearful man once prayed in Israel: "From the end of the earth I call to thee, when my heart is faint. Lead thou me to the rock that is higher than I; for thou art my refuge, a strong tower against the enemy. Let me dwell in thy tent forever! Oh to be safe under the shelter of thy wings" (Ps. 61, 2-4). Only God can be our refuge in the anguish of death. In extreme moments like that, God permits us to see what things are all about. He describes us as a child who is not wanted by his father and mother, but is rejected by them. Somewhere along the line we have been cast aside as foundlings. Our condition is described as that of a child who was not washed when it was born or covered with clothing. No one had pity on us; we were of no concern to anyone. And thus we were discarded like refuse on a dump. And then, God says: "And when I passed by you, and saw you weltering in your blood, I said to you in your blood, 'Live, and grow up like a plant of the field.' And you grew up and became tall and arrived at full maidenhood. . . ."(Ez. 16, 6). These are the figures that God uses to impress what the covenant should mean to man. This is an indication of how much he loves us in the covenant.

The most beautiful love we know is the noble love of a strong, devoted husband for his wife, the love of a man who continues in his love even when he notices that his wife has been unfaithful to him. This is the imagery that God uses to describe his love for us, with these words: "You must dwell as mine for many days . . . without belonging to another; so will I also be to you."

God calls us his allotted heritage (Deut. 32, 9). We all remember how happy we were with our first watch, our first bicycle, our first car. We polished and cared for them, so that they literally sparkled like diamonds. We would not think of lending them to anyone else. How concerned a person can be about his personal possessions even though they are only material things! And anyone who has ever received a person as a gift remembers how happy he was. When a young man finds a young woman for whom he may care, whom he may love, and by whom he is loved in turn, how concerned he becomes about her! How jealous he is in regard to her when he becomes aware that henceforth she will really be his. The same is naturally true on her part also. She will begin to look on him as her most priceless treasure; God has apparently created them for each other. In like manner we are God's personal possession. It is foolishness to imagine that God would ever abandon us. "Can a woman forget her sucking child?" he says. "Yet I will not forget you" (Is. 49, 15). "I am with you, always, to the close of the age" (Mt. 28, 20).

An eagle builds its nest high in the mountains. When its young have grown sufficiently so that they are capable of leaving the nest, they spread their wings and hop up and away from the nest. But the adult eagle, knowing the heights and knowing his young, flies after them. He sees them tire, and he sees them sink, but they do not fall far because with his mighty wings he supports the young animal. This is the way the bible describes the relationship between God and us in the covenant (Deut. 32, 11).

This relationship is described in yet another manner. In the Near East danger is constantly present for grazing and for straying sheep. This danger lies waiting on the steppes and in the crevices of the rocks. It threatens not only the animals but also the shepherd. A starving wolf can also attack him. A hireling flees and abandons his sheep to save his own life. But God is the good shepherd who gives his life for his sheep (Jn. 10, 11). These are some of the ideas that the holy scriptures use to impress us with the reality of the covenant.

The Two Partners of the Covenant

Human society would be impossible if we could not rely on each other. A man's life would be a living hell if every day when he came back from work he would have to ask if his wife were still there. No child can be happy and grow up wholesomely if it does not have the security that a father and mother will care for him. This point is well made by a poster against divorce in which a child is pictured as saying: "Think of me." We could take no pleasure in our work if we were not certain that we will be rewarded for it and that it has interior worth apart from the salary. We must be able to rely on each other. This is the reason for labor contracts, for the promise of fidelity in matrimony, for treaties with other peoples. Such an agreement, such a covenant, such a treaty gives us the security which we need in order to live. Without mutual trust, life would be hell. By an agreement, a covenant, or a pact, a man knows exactly where he stands. Whether this is a marriage contract, a religious profession, or a business agreement, it gives the assurance that we may expect something from the other and that he may expect something from us. The concern is mutual not only in love, but in any alliance. When a husband promises fidelity to his wife, she must also promise him hers. If either one of them fails, there results a situation which can have dire consequences. If someone agrees with his employer that he will receive a certain salary, the employer also must have the assurance that his employee will produce a certain amount of work. If the employee fails, he is threatened with dismissal; if the employer fails, he is threatened with a strike.

When at the consecration of the wine Christ said: "This cup is the new covenant in my blood," he recalled to the apostles' minds the whole world of the old covenant as we described it above. There appeared before their mind's eye the image of Mount Sinai with all that had transpired there. They heard God say: "I will be your God" (Lev. 26, 12). In these words they heard God's part of the covenant: he pledged himself to care for his people as a shepherd for his flock, as a husband for his wife, as a mother for her child. Nothing would ever be wanting, because he himself would lead his people to the green pastures of the promised land.

On the other hand the apostles also heard the response of Israel: "All that the Lord has spoken we will do and we will be obedient" (Exod. 24, 7). These words outline their whole obligation, their faith in God, their trust in him, their love toward him, their obedience to his law and the fulfillment of his desires.

All this is called to mind with Jesus' use of the word "covenant." As a matter of fact, its connotation was still wider. It alluded to the prophet Hosea who appeared at the time when Israel was neglecting its covenant relationship to God. This prophet was prepared for his difficult task by God in a peculiarly dramatic fashion. God permitted this man to experience personally what God was experiencing with his people. The covenant between God and Israel was comparable to a marriage contract. In marriage, love must come from both sides. And Israel had actually become unfaithful to God.

Something of the same sort happened in the life of Hosea. He had a wife whom he loved dearly. But in spite of his great love for her, in spite of his great care for her, she deserted him in a most despicable manner. Can there be greater consternation for a man than when he begins to notice that his wife loves no longer him and that a third person has entered her life and has replaced him? Yet Hosea forgave her and took her back. Because of this experience he sensed the gravity of the task God gave him. He was to restore the marriage between Yahweh and his people. He was to show Israel that it failed in its obligation, that it was unfaithful. No one can do this better than he who has experienced a similar situation in his own life; such a person can be an authentic intercessor for God. It is as though he is speaking to his own children, as though God were saying to the children of Israel: "Plead with your mother, plead—for she is not my wife, and I am not her husband—that she put away her harlotry from her face and her adultery from between her breasts" (Hos. 2, 2).

With these words Yahweh proclaims the divorce. But it is not permanent; the door remains open, there is a way back because Yahweh loves his unfaithful wife in spite of all. He follows her the way Hosea followed his own wife. And when Yahweh finds her, he says: "You must dwell as

mine for many days; you shall not play the harlot or belong to another man; so will I also be to you" (Hos. 3, 3).
All these Old Testament associations are hinted at with the
word "covenant" which Jesus used. There is an obvious
conclusion: God does not fail. His love is eternal. But in
the covenant—and especially in the new covenant—this
love must be mutual. If God finds his people again in the
new covenant, he repeats, so to speak, the words of
Hosea: "Dwell as mine for many days . . . belong to no
other man." This is a new and eternal covenant in which
men promise their fidelity and where they are given the
assurance that the blood is shed for the remission of
sins.

The Eternal Covenant

To understand a man a person must know his past. This
is a rule of thumb used by every psychologist and every
spiritual director. That is the way it should be. One will,
for example, judge differently the anxiety of a person
when one learns that as a child he experienced a bomb
raid. This rule of thumb is applicable in its way in every
field. Whoever would understand Communism must ac-
quaint himself with the social situation of the previous
century, with its child labor, fourteen-hour workday,
degenerating poverty and enormous wealth. It is equally
applicable to the work of Christ. The new covenant in-
augurated by him can be understood only against the
background of the old covenant. Various prophets were
compelled to attest that circumstances in the old covenant
were intolerable. They were constantly confronted by the
infidelity of the people. Such a situation could not prevail.
Gradually there arose the insight that something new had
to come—a new covenant which would be eternal, in
which mutual fidelity between God and man would be
guaranteed.

There is no doubt that at the Last Supper Christ and the apostles thought of the promise made by the prophet Jeremiah: "Behold, the days are coming, says the Lord, when I will make a new covenant with the house of Israel and the house of Judah, not like the covenant which I made with their fathers . . . which they broke. . . . But this is the covenant I will make with the house of Israel after those days, says the Lord: I will put my law within them, and I will write it upon their hearts. . . . I will forgive their iniquity, and I will remember their sin no more" (Jer. 31, 31-34).

How has this been accomplished? It is obvious that Christians cannot pretend that they are the faithful people of God. Whoever is mindful of the failings of both Christianity and Christians will not admit such a thought. Are we then still waiting for the fulfillment of Jeremiah's prophecy? We do not think so.

Christ said at the Last Supper: "This is *the new covenant*." Where then is the eternal fidelity on man's part? The answer to this question is in all probability given by Isaiah. In any event he also asked this question. He also realized that such an ideal race of man did not exist and perhaps cannot exist. We can detect something striking in all his prophecies. He sees all men, as it were, melting together into one man. He does not yet know what this man should be called; he calls him "the servant of Yahweh." And then he prophesies something which no one would have believed: he sees the new and eternal covenant actualized in one person. He names that person the "covenant": "I have taken you by the hand . . . and I have given you as a covenant to the people" (Is. 42, 6). Elsewhere he writes: "Thus says the Lord: In a time of favor . . . I have . . . given you as a covenant to the people" (Is. 49, 8).

This is something truly noteworthy: the whole covenant in *one* person. One is inclined to say that a covenant always presupposes at least two persons. Thus when there is a question of a covenant between God and man, one must presuppose that there will be two partners in this covenant—God and man. In this covenant there must be present the loving, forgiving God on one hand and an obedient, loving, submissive man on the other. Yet in Isaiah we read that the covenant was made in one person.

This is what actually happened. Jesus Christ is the one who in his person possesses both God's love and man's loving response. Christ said: "Who sees me, sees the Father." Here we have the descending line of the covenant, the line coming from God. God's part is visible. In Christ we can really see God's love; whoever wants to know what God's love is can see this in Christ. There God's love has acquired a human, visible form. In Christ, God's love for man, his willingness to forgive, his pity on the poor, the sick, the sinners, and the bunglers, becomes tangible and apparent. Christ is indeed the savior, the Lord, the redeemer; in him is salvation. He is the assurance that God is benevolent.

Yet there is more in Christ. The ascending line is also present in his person and becomes visible in his actions. In him has come the ideal man, the man wholly faithful to the promise. He is the man in whose heart the law of God is written, who takes God's law seriously. It is his food and drink to accomplish the will of the Father. He prayed: "Not my will but thine be done" (Lk. 22, 42). In the desert he relived Israel's history anew with all the hardships and temptations which the Israelites had experienced. In contrast with the ancient Israel, however, he said "No" to all the temptations. That is the way Christ was here on earth; that is the way he is in eternity. That is why he is the covenant. That is why this covenant is eternal and yet always new.

To what extent this covenant will be eternal for the rest of mankind depends upon the manner in which they identify themselves with Christ. This thus becomes a matter of importance—to be incorporated in Christ, to become one with him. Only then is the covenant eternal for man.

Entering the Covenant

It is generally not a simple matter for a foreigner to become a naturalized citizen of a particular country with all the rights, advantages and protection this involves. It costs much money and involves many formalities.

In the period of Israel's origin the case was much the same, though probably somewhat less bureaucratic. In that period there were many tribes who regarded themselves as their own nationality. Even today there are cases in Africa or New Guinea, for instance, where the member of a strange tribe cannot possibly feel secure among another tribe. He must first be adopted by that tribe. One might say he must first acquire the nationality of the other tribe. This entailed various ceremonies at the time of Israel's origin. If one wanted to be adopted into a tribe, one had to become a member of one of the families of that tribe. As a matter of fact each tribe was really an extension of the family. A sort of blood relationship was thus required to belong to a tribe. Whoever had the same blood belonged to the tribe; he was absolutely safe among them and enjoyed all the privileges of hospitality and protection. To establish such a blood relationship, use was often made of a sort of primitive blood transfusion. A person would apply to himself several drops of blood given by someone else. In this manner the covenant was concluded. One became a blood relation in the most literal sense of the word. Occasionally the ceremonial was simpler. The head of the tribe could permit the stranger to eat of his own food. The latter was then regarded as a blood relative. Both had partaken of the same food and the same drink. The body of each had absorbed the same food; they were thus one. One could not any longer become angry at the other; to wish evil to someone who had eaten from the same table was something horrible. It was equivalent to wishing evil to one's blood relative.

God made the Jewish people his blood relations in this manner. After he had made the arrangements with the Jewish people, he permitted them to partake of the food and the drink which they offered to him. Such eating and drinking was a confirmation of the covenant. By partaking of God's food and drink man becomes God's blood relation and acknowledges himself one with God. Instead of signing a ream of papers and formulae as we do, these people simply ate and drank what God offered them. By doing so they belonged to God's people and to his family.

Something new has happened since then. The old covenant between God and man ran amuck because of man's infidelity. We know that God in a wonderful manner renewed the old covenant so that it is now secure, that it can never be broken again. The new covenant is absolutely eternal. No man is able to change it. In Jesus Christ, man and God are irrevocably bound with each other in close covenant. And although God made the covenant with Jesus Christ, and with him alone, we can all nevertheless participate in this covenant. This happens through baptism and the eucharist: by baptism a man enters into Christ; in the eucharist this unity grows to immeasurable profundity.

As a stranger became a blood relation in former times by eating the food which the tribal head offered him, so we become a blood relative of Christ by eating the food which is given to us in communion. This is a true entry into Christ, with all its consequences. And these consequences are that God regards us as his own children and that he loves us as he loved Christ. Thus it follows that after holy communion God says to us: "You are my beloved child; do not fear; I am your Father." And thus we have the assurance that we are living in the new and eternal covenant with God.

It is obvious that this also has its consequences in our thinking and acting. We may summarize it as follows: We must be governed by the same disposition that prevailed in Jesus Christ, who always said to the Father: "Not my will, but thine be done" (Lk. 22, 42).

Fidelity to the Covenant

One of the reasons why the old covenant failed, in a sense, was undoubtedly its formalism, its automatic aspect. Many Jews thought that everything was in order between God and themselves when they observed the law of circumcision and offered God an animal from time to time; then God should be well satisfied.

The prophets already saw that this mentality was untenable. The point is not what they say about the character of the sacrifices, but about the dispositions with which they were offered. Thus the psalmist has God say: "I do not reprove you for your sacrifices; your burned offerings are continually before me. I will accept no bull from your house, nor he-goat from your folds. For every beast of the forest is mine, the cattle on a thousand hills. . . . If I were hungry I would not tell you, for the world and all that is in it is mine. Do I eat the flesh of bulls, or drink the blood of goats? . . . Pay rather your vows to the Most High; then I will deliver you, and you will glorify me" (Ps. 50, 8-15).

We also run the risk of appealing to the eternal character of the covenant under which we are living. It is eternal but it is so only because Christ is eternally faithful to God. Whether the covenant will have an eternal character for every Christian depends upon whether his life conforms to the covenant and its conditions. Naturally, we do not wish to portray God as a solemn old man whose favor must be curried by careful service. Yet the danger is always there that we perform or fulfill a certain number of our obligations and then think that somehow or other God ought to be satisfied. We know what the law of the new and eternal covenant demands. This law has been clearly stated by Jesus at the Last Supper. It says: "Love one another, even as I have loved you," and "By this shall all men know that you are my disciples, if you love one another" (Jn. 13, 34-35).

When the Jews had made their covenant with God they offered him a gift. They even gave him a very precious gift: they gave the best of their fields and of their flock. It was a token of their sincerity. With these gifts they wanted to say: "God, we will do everything you have asked; we pledge this with all our being and our goods. You can count on this; here is our guarantee."

In the new covenant the situation is different, more important, and permanent. The guarantee has been given by Christ. When he offered himself he was wholly one with us. He gave himself in this condition; he offered his life as assurance that mankind would be faithful to God. It can therefore readily be understood how terrible it would be if the Lord's Church would not be faithful to her commission. It would in a certain sense frustrate the redemption. In his boundless confidence Christ dared to make himself the guarantor of our fidelity to the covenant; yet it lies within our power to let the covenant fail as far as we are concerned.

By receiving holy communion we enter into Christ; we come into contact with him and form an alliance. Nonetheless this must be made actual by establishing a clear bond between our worship and our lives.

The Offering

It seems apropos here in this chapter to add a few words about the meaning of the offering. In his better moments every man senses that his life does not come from himself but from God. In these moments a man feels that he must somehow or other acknowledge and demonstrate this conviction externally. There has been no period of time when man has not approached God with a gift. Obviously this attitude persists in our liturgy.

More than once we have already intimated that the worship of God is impossible without the service of men. This becomes all the more evident when man reaches the climax of his worship, the moment when he wishes to bring a gift to God. At this moment his love of neighbor must also find its acme.

Never was a greater gift offered God than when Christ brought his. For all eternity it will remain the sole sufficing sacrifice. With this gift God was offered not only the greatest of all worship; it was also the greatest expression of love for mankind because it was offered for the salvation of the whole world.

This example of the Lord is imitated in the Offertory procession. It is well known how in former times Christians offered their gifts. They were well aware that the only sufficing sacrifice was that of Christ. On the other hand they also understood that this did not give them permission to be passive. That is why they came with their gifts at the eucharistic celebrations. With these gifts they wanted to say: "God, we want to be associated with the offering of our Lord; we want to make it our offering too; we want to be part of it." At the same time the Offertory procession was an exercise of love of neighbor, because the gifts that were brought were destined for people in need, for the sick, for the weak and the destitute.

Perhaps it is regrettable that the Offertory procession in this form has practically disappeared. It could not be otherwise, because the number of Christians grew constantly and so did the nature of the gifts presented. That is the reason why money began to be substituted for gifts.

Unfortunately, there is nothing as noncommittal and cold as money. It stands to reason that it is hard to see the aspect of sacredness in the collection. Yet the collection must be viewed in this light: as an offering to God and an expression of love toward our neighbor.

If the collection is not seen in this light, then it becomes worthless as a religious act and meaningless as an expression of love for neighbor. In that case also those who have charge of the church buildings, the sick, the poor, might be compromised. It will become impossible to supply those who are in need and to give them the help they need.

Although a solution was sought, we are not happy about one solution that has been commonly adopted—that is, the taking of several collections according to the principle that, if one collection produces one dollar, six collections will produce six times as much. It is obvious that this is a financial, a materialistic solution to an essentially religious problem. Such a problem can be solved only in a religious fashion, by revitalizing the understanding that the worship of God presupposes the love of man. The question here is not one of externals. It pertains to the heart of the matter. This action must also be a symbol by which we express the mentality that prevails among us.

When we go to visit a friend we take along something for his wife or his children. Everyone senses that this gift is basically a gift to the friend. When a child misbehaves while we are visiting, the child is reprimanded. Doesn't it often happen in such a case that the visitor assumes the role of advocate in behalf of the child and says: "Oh, he didn't mean it; he didn't know what he was doing." The same thing happens in the eucharist. There we intend to honor the Father by offering gifts to his children. There we desire to please the Father by granting pardon to his children.

CHAPTER FIVE

The Lord's Supper

A Meal as a Symbol of Love

Whenever we speak of the eucharist as the Lord's supper it is well to note at once that there is no question here of satisfying the appetite. Furthermore all of us will readily grant that such satisfaction is not the first intention of a solemn banquet as it is known in our daily practice, as on the occasion of a farewell or a jubilee or a wedding. On such occasions we gather round the table not primarily to satisfy our hunger, but to assemble in love and fellowship. A banquet is shot through with bonds of love; it serves well as a symbol of loving fellowship. At a farewell banquet we express our regard for our departing loved one. On the other hand, a banquet offered by the departing person is a clear sign of his love for us.

This is also the way God acts. When he wants to express his love for man, he often speaks of a wedding banquet. The kingdom of heaven is frequently represented under the image of a festive banquet. This is an obvious symbol of the unity and the relationship which will exist in the kingdom of heaven between God and us, and among ourselves.

Even God's love for sinners is described under the imagery of a banquet. This will be one of the blessings of the final era. God will step forward to greet sinners with mercy. This is actually what happened in Christ. He ate with sinners and publicans. For the proud Jews who thought they could please God with their own righteousness this was the cause of great scandal, and they let Christ know about it. Christ's answer was typically messianic; he offered no excuse whatever for eating with sinners and publicans. On the contrary, he replied that that was precisely why he had come. Christ is here implicitly alluding to the many messianic texts of the holy scriptures which describe the salvation of the final era, concerning which it was said: "The poor shall eat and be filled."

It will perhaps be beneficial here to expand a little on the relationship between sin and communion. In the past, the purity demanded for communion was overemphasized. Communion was regarded as the reward for a pure life rather than an appeal to the forgiver of sins. In point of fact there is a sin that excommunicates us, having as its result exclusion from communion because this sin signifies a separation from God. But what kind of a sin is this, which we call mortal? In what follows it is by no means our intention to paint white what is black, but we cannot escape the impression that in the past some unconsidered things were said concerning mortal sin. Furthermore, it cannot be denied that for a long time a man was judged exclusively by his external deeds and that these deeds were not considered sufficiently in relation to his interiority. Yet it is absolutely necessary to know the mentality of a person in order to exercise correct judgment over his deeds.

It seems best to us to start from the fellowship consideration. Between God and man there exists a relationship of love. On his part God loves man; he has a high regard for man, as is evident from the incarnation and many other noble deeds. On the other hand, many a person can say honestly that he has a deep regard for God. This must naturally be qualified with the proper restrictions, because every man often fails in the manifestation of his

love. Nevertheless, in spite of these many failures, most
people can say honestly that they have a regard for God.
It is thus manifestly a mutual regard of love, which can
be compared to the relationship of parents to children, or
that of a husband to his wife. Mortal sin is a rupture in
this relationship of love between God and man. We are
fully justified in comparing this with other relationships of
love, when there is a break in the relations between parents and child, between husband and wife.

It cannot be denied that even in the best marriages
there will occasionally arise an unpleasant situation, a
serious difference in opinion, when one or the other does
something that is definitely offensive to the other party.
This however does not automatically lead to a break. A
break *can* occur, but much more is required for this. It
could occur, for example, if one would completely ignore
the other without any consideration for the desires and
needs of the other, without ever doing anything for the
other, without ever having any regard for the other. If the
one or the other is living in such a situation, then indeed
an offensive action can cause a break. But normally speaking, when the relationship is a good one, when there is
some consideration for the other, some regard or concern,
some account for his desires, when in such a situation the
same offensive action occurs, it acquires an entirely different aspect and will be judged in a different manner.

All this can be fully applied to our relationship with
God. Here, too, from time to time something will occur
which is not in order. But this does not necessarily mean a
rupture. A break can occur when one totally ignores God
without any concern about him at all, without any regard
for his desires. Such would be the case if one would never
speak to him in prayer, would always disregard him, especially in one's fellowmen. It would then be only natural
that a specific action would, in fact, cause a break. But
when one has the right intention toward God, and mani-

fests this by communing with him in honest prayer, by doing something meaningful for another, by performing his tasks as well as possible, by actively participating in the eucharist, by being patient and helpful toward one's fellowman—in short, if one directs his life toward God and toward his fellowman—then the whole affair assumes a different aspect. Whoever is thus intentioned toward God does not break his relation with him without further ado; this is a psychological impossibility. Let us suppose that someone is living such a kind of life, but finds particular circumstances so difficult that he can no longer resist and actually "falls." There is no question of mortal sin. The fear which one meets occasionally in people that after trying all their lives to do their best they may still run a chance of committing a mortal sin just before their death and thus lose their souls is totally unfounded.

Many find it difficult to judge properly in their own affairs. Many live in fear, uncertainty and anguish of conscience. The reason for this can often be placed in a wrong insight or in a faulty judgment. A serious discussion with a conscientious priest or a knowing layman will generally be helpful. It is also certain that the conscience of many has been formed one-sidedly from their early youth. The number of people for whom there seems to be only one sin, the one against sex, is still extraordinarily large. And even here there are misunderstandings. It is impossible within the limits of this book to give a full answer to the many questions that exist. However, we would like to emphasize that psychology teaches us to judge somewhat more leniently the difficulties encountered in puberty or the behavior of a man who is either temporarily or perhaps permanently subject to great tension. In like manner, judgment concerning people with an abnormal sexual life must be quite nuanced and thus very mild.

Concerning the outlook of the Church on married life

and allied problems it seems to us that we may safely say that her message should consist primarily in teaching that marriage is both a privilege and an obligation. The obligation consists in a readiness for mutual fidelity and noble fertility. This noble fertility must be responsible to and in accord with the social circumstances, the health and the educational capabilities of the married couple. These circumstances will often make a responsible spacing of children obligatory. It is our conviction that concerning this matter the parents must themselves reach a responsible decision after they have consulted the opinion of some other conscientious Christian. As for the means to be used in spacing, the answer of a concerned and loving Church will have to be that every means used must be an aid toward the increase of their fellowship in love. Furthermore, it is obvious that many aids contain certain disadvantages and that it will thus be frequently necessary to choose the lesser of two evils.

We are convinced that here lie many concrete difficulties that have caused people to leave the Church or stop receiving holy communion. Unfortunately it is possible to touch these difficulties only in passing. These generalities will have to suffice here with the admonition that the reader consult other sources where these difficulties are treated in detail and where it will appear that these problems that are the concern of so many people are being considered with a much more balanced light. This does not mean that everything has become easier, but that the accent is being placed on other considerations which make the whole problem more balanced.

What we did want to say in this regard is that we must be very careful in pronouncing the guilt of mortal sin either upon ourselves or upon others. It happens time and time again that people who are disquieted about having broken with God expect treatment from God different from that which they extend toward their children. When they are asked: "Would you send such a child out of your home if he had done the same thing as you did?" they immediately give the absolute answer: "No, I would take him closer to myself." If we, then, who are evil, know how to give good gifts to our children, how much more will our Father, who is in heaven and infinitely good, do so with us (Mt. 7, 11)? It is indeed difficult to acquire a correct and independent conscience. Yet we think it is useful to have formulated the above principles. They will perhaps be of some help.

Let us repeat again that it is not our intention to hush-hush all sins. We only want to point out that for a break with God we must not consider the action as much as the mentality. Sin is wanting in no human life, but this need not prevent anyone from eating with Christ, particularly since he came precisely for sinners and is known to have eaten with sinners. In a certain sense it may be said that the eucharist presupposes our sinfulness because it is *the* sacrament for the forgiveness of sin. We are not merely mouthing empty formulae when before communion we say "Lord, I am *not* worthy" and "Behold, the lamb of God, who takes away the sins of the world." In like manner it is not an empty formula when in the words of consecration it is said that the blood was shed for the *forgiveness of sins.* There is a sentence in the first Epistle of John which is possibly not sufficiently known: "By this we shall know that we are of the truth, and reassure our hearts before him whenever our hearts condemn us; for God is greater than our hearts, and he knows everything" (1 Jn. 3, 19).

At the Lord's supper one thing is asked unconditionally of all those who partake: they must be filled with love. Lack of love cannot be tolerated at this table. In a home a naughty child is dismissed from table. Many a person has experienced in his own life that it is impossible to eat when there is contention during the meal. It is a medical fact that food eaten when a person is disturbed causes indigestion. Thus we are advised to wait in such a situation until the tension is over.

The history of David teaches us clearly how the bible considers it almost a sacrilege to share in a meal with someone with whom we are in discord. When David was persecuted and had to hide in caves because his life was not safe and an attack was plotted against him, he laid his grief before God. It is noteworthy that he lets God see the greatness of his grief by saying that he is persecuted by someone who sat at his table and with whom he had eaten sweetbreads. This is what hurts him. A man had given him a token, a symbol of love, by eating with him. Actually it had been a misuse of the symbolic value of the meal.

So also in the life of Jesus it is obvious how concerned he is about sharing a meal without sharing love. When Christ was alluding to Judas as the traitor he said: "One of you will betray me, one who is eating with me" (Mk. 14, 18). In this episode of Mark's gospel we have a dramatic presentation of how Christ was hurt by the fact that Judas was also partaking in this meal of love (Mk. 14, 17-21).

Whoever celebrates the eucharist must remember that this banquet necessarily presupposes love. It is not by accident that on the occasion of this supper the Lord proclaimed his great commandment of love. Love is the high point of all the commandments, and the high point of worship is the Lord's supper. Thus we come again, albeit by a different route, to a conclusion that we have drawn before: there is a bond between religion and life, between the worship of God and the service of man. These two high points concur in the eucharist! To celebrate the eucharist is the same as being one with the Lord and with each other, to communicate with the Lord and with fellowmen, to grow in unity. In this manner, and especially in this manner, will unity among men be effected. This unity is in fact becoming more and more a reality, though we are still far from its full realization.

Yet it must be said that whoever studies the history of mankind seriously becomes an optimist. To him it will become unmistakably clear that throughout the course of history there is a growth of unity. There was a time when the world was inhabited by tribes totally independent of each other. The ancient Germanic peoples had no idea about the Inca culture of South America. They had never heard of each other, and thus were not concerned about each other. Yet gradually and surely the world became smaller. Tribes were united into countries and countries were united into continents. Today we are surrounded by examples of unity of which no one could have dreamed a few centuries ago—the United Nations, the European Common Market, etc. There is simply no doubt about it; the world is growing toward unity.

In religion, too, we see a growth toward unity. Our times are buzzing with the word "ecumenical." Most of us remember the time when the various religions were hostile to each other. We did not understand each other because we never listened to each other. Now a conversation has begun which cannot be stopped. We have reached the point where we are listening to each other; here and there we are even beginning to understand each other. We are finding among each other undeniable traces of Christ. We are getting the impression that Christ's prayer "That they may all be one" (Jn. 17, 21) is actually being answered. This is Christ's most ardent desire. He prayed insistently for unity; he worked hard for unity. The sacrament he left behind is the sacrament of unity. The longing that we all experience sitting in intimate unity at the Lord's table in the company of our separated brothers and sisters is unquenchable. This was the ideal of our Lord.

It is in this sacrament that the Church gets her proper image. It is in this sacrament that the unity of the Church is brought about. For here, all are gathered together around one loaf and one cup. Here we approach the foremost symbol of unity—a meal. If unity is accomplished anywhere, it is at a meal. No householder tolerates discord during the meal. In the eucharistic banquet we come in contact with the Lord who is the "cornerstone uniting the different walls."

By eating his body we become one body of which he is the head. By eating with each other we eat for each other, as when we drink a toast to each other's health. No wonder that it was at this eucharistic banquet that Christ used the image of the vine and the branches. The vine is not a separate pole standing alongside the stock to hold it up, the way tomato plants are supported with a stick. The vine is the whole plant, including branches and roots. "I am the vine," he said; "you are the branches." A more intimate unity can hardly be imagined. The same life flows throughout the whole plant. No branch possesses life independently of the vine just as no twig has life independently of the tree. "Abide in me, and I [will abide] in you. . . ." (Jn. 15, 4). "He who eats my flesh . . . abides in me, and I in him" (Jn. 6, 57).

St. Paul attempts to clarify this unity be using a different figure, that of a body. Head and members are one; they cannot do without each other. They cannot fight with each other; they need each other. The hand cannot grasp what is distant if the feet do not bring it there (1 Cor. 12, 12ff.).

Humanity tends toward unity. But humanity will achieve authentic and intimate unity only when all are gathered round the one table of the Lord. We must ever keep before our eyes this eschatological character of the eucharist as the supreme ideal which will be achieved at the end of time. The Church understood from the very first that her unity would be effected by and through this meal. This was the reason underlying the custom of sending to other churches some of the bread consecrated at the pope's Mass. This was to emphasize the necessity for unity.

It was not without reason that St. Paul was so disturbed about the dissensions manifested at the eucharistic banquet at Corinth: "It is not the Lord's supper that you eat" (1 Cor. 11, 20). This is also the reason why in the prayers of the eucharist the plural is used: we offer, we eat, we thank, we commemorate. That is why we celebrate the eucharist in unity with the pope and the bishops and commemorate those who are not present. We are conscious of being associated with the saints and with all the faithful departed. Wherever the eucharist is celebrated, unity is either presupposed or effected. If this aspect is not taken seriously, if men sit together at the eucharistic table while they foster discord at their home table, the Lord's supper loses its authenticity. Such action also obstructs the growth of unity in the world.

Christ's Presence

From early youth we have been told about Christ's presence under the appearance of bread and wine. Many ask how Christ is present in the bread and wine. Starting out from the data of faith that Christ is truly present (and on this point there is no doubt for a believing Catholic), it is possible—and will also be helpful toward a greater intensity of our faith—to consider the manner of this presence.

It is certain that in the eucharist we are dealing with a different manner of presence than, for instance, the presence of water in a glass. If Christ were present under the appearances of bread and wine in this manner, then the accusation made against us centuries ago would indeed be true: we would be like cannibals eating human flesh.

Christ, however, is present in a different way. But how? We use the term "sacramental presence." It is our opinion that it is possible to clarify this mystery somewhat.

In the first place it should be noted that there are many ways in which a person can be present somewhere. There is the presence of water in a glass. This is the least meaningful way of being present. It is a wholly material presence like soup in a plate or potatoes in a pan. It is the presence of thousands of persons in a city; they are there all right, but they are not present for each other. It is mere physical occupancy, and nothing more.

Richer and more meaningful is the presence of a mother who telephones her child in the hospital. Though she is not materially in the room, yet she is really there. She is there much more so than if she were physically present in the room but showed no interest. If a person were to ask such a child: "Who called you?" he would certainly not get the answer: "That was the voice of my mother." The child would simply say: "That *was* my mother."

A symbolic presence can be yet richer. We refer here to what was said earlier concerning symbols. As an example we may recall the symbolism and the presence of President John Kennedy in the flag which was given to his wife during his funeral. In like manner our country is present to us in our flag. No one looks upon this pennant as a mere piece of linen; this is obvious from the fact that every country is deeply insulted when someone tears or soils its flag.

The presence of God in the eucharist is a sacramental one. It is difficult if not impossible to express this in ordinary human words; after all, we are dealing with a mystery. But we can approach this mystery by the use of symbol-concepts, because the sacraments are basically symbolic acts. It is important to define our notion of "symbol" carefully. In our daily speech the remark is often made: "Oh, that's merely symbolic"—as if to say: "It is not gen-

uine; it is only a reflection of reality." This is not the real
meaning of the word "symbol."

We have an almost innate abhorrence for empty, hol-
low, unreal symbols which do not contain the reality they
symbolize. The thing symbolized must be present in the
symbol. When we share our sympathy with someone, we
do not like to use the word "condolence" because this
word is used too much and thus has acquired a loose,
threadbare meaning. We try to find words—and we are
best aware of this when we try to write a real letter of
condolence—which will better express our authentic feeling. This is why we would much rather say in situations of
this sort: "You know what I mean; I find it so hard to put
it into words."

When on some occasion someone congratulates us with
a loose, weak, disinterested handshake, we feel mocked.
It is an empty gesture, a meaningless symbol, and thus no
symbol at all. What should be symbolized is not there.
The man behind the handshake is not in it. The living
symbol must be filled with something of the one who
presents it. When one sympathizes with another because
of a great loss, then something of this condolence must
form part of the handshake. When before her final de-
parture a mother gives a remembrance to each of her
children, something of her love and concern for her children is contained in this token.

Is this also the case with the eucharist? This is the general idea, but the eucharist goes further, much further, for
it becomes a sacramental symbol. Nonetheless we could
also say that if the eucharist were not a sacrament,
Christ's love and care for us would still be present in that
bread. But now the God-man, the ideal man, the man par
excellence, the perfect man, gives us this symbol. Where
we, as imperfect men, are capable of expressing ourselves
in only an imperfect manner, he, the perfect man, can
express himself perfectly.

What we are trying to say can be grasped more clearly by the example of a mother feeding her child. Biologically speaking she perhaps gives her child no more than certain chemical elements; in reality, however, with the milk of her breast she gives her mother's love. When a father works all day to fill the mouths of his children, then something of him is present in the food. When a young man hands his girl a piece of pastry, in reality he gives her more than what is on the table; he gives her part of his love. It has often been noticed that people who live alone pay little attention to their meals, but when they have visitors they prepare a banquet fit for a king; then they try to give part of themselves to the other.

All these examples show how the symbol becomes authentic only by being filled with part of what is being symbolized. We thus come to realize that the host in some sense gives himself in the food he offers his guests. In our human symbols, however, there is always an element of imperfection. No host can ever identify himself wholly with the food; no host can ever become actual food.

In the sacrament of the eucharist this imperfection has been removed. Here the human symbol has evolved to its absolute perfection. What is hinted at in each human symbol but never realized finds its fulfillment here. At every commemoration we want to make the past present. But we never succeed fully. By her anxious activity a mother wants to share her love, but she can never do this wholly. However, when the Lord offers us the bread of heaven, it contains not just part of his love, but all his love. He is himself present. Here the symbol has become a *perfect* one.

The liturgy is deeply convinced of this reality. Pointing at the bread, it says in a concrete manner: "Behold here, the lamb of God, who takes away the sins of the world." Christ says, just as realistically: "This is my body." At the distribution of holy communion the priest says: "The body of Christ," and we answer: "Amen." This word means: "I believe."

Mutual Love

A symbol is never used aimlessly; it is always directed toward another person. It presupposes that the other will respond. There must thus be an answer; if this is not so, then the kiss dies on the lips. Then the symbol of love fades away because it has been given in vain, because it has been destroyed. Many a person can testify from his own experience how painful this is.

Perhaps we have experienced the painful refusal of a proffered hand. There was a disagreement and we wished to make amends. We gathered all our courage to set things right with the other person—and this can be very difficult at times. When we extended our hand to the other we gave him the symbol of all the goodwill and courage and effort we could muster. When the other person rejected this symbol, something irrevocable took place. The symbol did not reach maturity; it was cut off halfway, as though the hand had become paralyzed and frozen. Nothing is so distressing as the rejection of a symbol, because it is the rejection of what it symbolized, of the person himself.

Every symbol presupposes that the other will cooperate. An invitation must be accepted; where this is not the case the love which was present in the symbol wanes. An embrace which is refused becomes frozen. Someone who wracks his brain to find the proper words to express his condolence with a friend at his loss, and is then told to stop putting on airs, is deeply hurt. Sympathy ceases at that moment because the symbol of sympathy was refused. Perhaps some of us have experienced the unpleasant sensation of having spoken to someone who did not listen, but had his attention elsewhere. It becomes impossible to speak further with such a person.

Many a priest knows the unpleasantness of a sermon which was not listened to; even our Lord was not spared this experience. He felt it when he preached in Capharnaum; and after the multiplication of the loaves he addressed his apostles with profound disillusionment: "Will you go also away?" (Jn. 6, 67).

A symbol presupposes without doubt that the other will accept it. If this acceptance is missing, then the symbol fails to achieve its purpose. It immediately ceases to exist. But when a symbol is accepted and is given an answer, it is a cause of great joy. We know of the joy of giving a child something he wanted as a present. We enjoy seeing how the child forgets everything around him to drive his small car around the room. We rejoice because the symbol was accepted so intently.

Every gift is a symbol; yet this symbol reaches its full status only when the gift is admired. We wait for this admiration. Perhaps this is the underlying reason for wrapping a gift, so that the giver can see the wonderment when the gift is unwrapped. When someone sets aside an unwrapped gift, the symbol is broken; it ceases to exist. The gift is still there but its symbol is not. This again is the reason why it can be so painful when, after having gone from store to store to find something original for someone, we discover at the moment of the unwrapping that this person has already received exactly the same gift. Imagine the case when a person receives the twelfth tie as a gift. He will try to save the situation by saying that he is well pleased with it. Nevertheless the event cannot be saved because this person is not in a position to admire the symbol properly.

From all this it should be evident that, in the eucharist

also, love must come from two sides. In this meal God offers us his love. But when this love is not accepted, when there is no faith in the eucharist, or when this love is reciprocated in a cool or slovenly manner, then humanly speaking God's love itself must wane. Nothing is more painful than rejected love.

It is sad to note from Sunday to Sunday that thousands who believe in the Lord and call themselves Christian do not accept this symbol of his love by going to holy communion. Among men this would surely be the end of love, but we have the assurance that God's love for men cannot wane, in spite of our cool attitude and repeated refusals.

Meal and Word

We have already mentioned that the purpose of the eucharistic banquet is not to satiate our bodily appetites. It would be better to speak of a symbolic meal and a symbolic eating, in which the spoken word plays an important role.

This is not strange. Banquets held on festive occasions also have this characteristic. The actual eating occupies the least time. Such a banquet may last two or three hours whereas the actual eating is done in half an hour. The main accent is on the word, whether this be as conversation, as formal addresses, or in the singing of songs. The word determines the character of the meal.

There are different types of meals. A meal can be a farewell banquet, a wedding banquet, an anniversary, or a memorial for a departed person. The menu may very well be the same for all but the words spoken at the meal tell us what it is for. It can be discovered easily by sitting down and listening. It won't be long before someone will rise to speak. If he begins: "Honored jubilarian, our company thought it appropriate to honor you on this day," then you know that the banquet is being given on the occasion of a business jubilee. If on the contrary you hear the speaker say: "My dear young man, before you leave for Australia, we want to wish you well," then you know that this is a farewell banquet. The words will tell us what kind of a banquet it is.

This is also the case with the eucharist. Here, too, the word is decisive. Perhaps some may think that we are referring to the service of the Word in the Epistle and the Gospel; but that is not the word meant here. The word which determines the eucharist is the great table prayer spoken by the celebrant, beginning with the Preface. If we listen to this, we know at once that we are present at a memorial banquet, in which the motif of honor and gratitude plays the principal part.

An address at a banquet succeeds only when the listeners share the same sentiments as the speaker; they must all approve the content of the speech. If the speech concerns gratitude, then all the guests must be filled with gratitude. Everyone senses that a speech at a silver wedding anniversary is not fitting if the children cannot be honestly grateful for any concern manifested in their behalf by the parents who are celebrating this feast. Under such circumstances the speech had better be omitted because none of those present can agree with the motif of gratitude. In the table address accompanying the eucharist, which for the greatest part is a memorial address, the thoughts of gratitude, honor and praise form the principal motif. If this address is to succeed, then all present must be animated with sincere gratitude to God. Directly opposed to this is the sense of obligation with which many come to Mass. Whoever looks upon the Sunday obligation as a burdensome, unpleasant task cannot be a grateful man. If such people are present, the table talk of the celebrant cannot be fully successful.

In primitive Christianity there was no determined fixed

text for this. Justin describes the eucharistic table talk as an improvised address. The president spoke a word of thanksgiving as long and as well as he could.

We have now a determined text—the Canon. Unfortunately it must be said that this text is overburdened with prayers of petition which really do not belong here, and which we hope in the future will be assigned to a better and more appropriate place. We will not treat them here. On the other hand, in order to understand the memorial address to the greatest possible extent, we must consider the prefaces of the feast throughout the Church year. If we leave aside the prayers of petition, we arrive at a more uniform whole. Sketched in large lines the text would look something like this:

It is truly right and just,
proper and helpful toward salvation,
that we always and everywhere give thanks to you,
O Lord, holy Father,
almighty and eternal God,
through Christ our Lord.

For in your mercy and fidelity
you gave him as redeemer of the human race
when it was lost.
His truth will instruct the ignorant,
his holiness will justify sinners,
his power will support the weak.

Through the mystery of the incarnate Word
a new light of your glory has shone upon us,
so that we are filled with love for the invisible
now that you have become visible to us.

When your only-begotten Son
appeared in our mortal nature,
he restored us through the new light of immortality.

Through him you curb vice
and exalt the soul;
you grant virtue and reward to our bodily fasting.

Almighty God,
you deigned that the salvation of mankind
should be accomplished on the tree of the cross
in order that life might be restored
by the very instrument that brought death,
and that Satan, who conquered us through the tree,
might also be overcome by it,
through Christ our Lord.

We thank you, almighty Father,
because now our paschal lamb, Christ, is sacrificed.
He is the true lamb,
who has taken away the sins of the world;
he overcame death for us by dying himself,
and restored us to life by his resurrection.

He appeared openly to his disciples
after his resurrection,
and was taken up to heaven before their eyes
so that he might make us sharers in his divinity
and prepare a place for us in his Father's house.

We thank you,
almighty, eternal God,
that you willed to be a God of mankind.
We thank you also for the light of our eyes,
for the music we hear,
and for the works of our hands.

We bless you for all your gifts in Christ, our Lord,
who on the day before his passion
took bread in his holy and venerable hands,
raised his eyes to heaven,
to you, God, the almighty Father,

and gave thanks,
broke the bread and gave it to his disciples
with the words: Take and eat you all of this,
for this is my body, given for you.

In like manner after the meal
he took the chalice
in his holy and venerable hands.
Again giving thanks to you,
he gave it to his disciples
with the words: Take and drink you all of this,
for this is the cup of the new and eternal covenant
which shall be shed for you and all
for the forgiveness of sin.

As often as you do these things,
do them in memory of me.

Mindful, therefore, Lord,
of the holy passion, the resurrection from the dead,
and the glorious ascension
of Christ, your Son, our Lord,
we, your servants,
together with all your holy people,
offer to your supreme majesty
from your own gracious gifts
this pure, holy, and spotless victim,
the holy bread of eternal life
and the cup of eternal salvation.

We beg your majesty,
send us your Holy Spirit,
the Spirit who gives life
and renews and strengthens everything,
the power of Jesus Christ.
We implore you,
let these gifts be an authentic sign
of our service to you and to our fellowman.

Regard these gifts
with gracious and kindly attention;
hold them acceptable as you accepted
the oblation of your just servant, Abel,
the sacrifice of our patriarch, Abraham,
and the holy offerings
of your high priest Melchisedech.
We humbly implore you,
bid your angels to bring this gift
to your heavenly altar,
in the presence of your divine majesty.
And may all of us who receive from this altar
the body and blood of your Son
be filled with all heavenly blessing,
through Christ, our Lord,
through whom you have created and sanctified all these gifts,
endowed them with life, blessed them and given them to us.
Through him, with him, and in him
is to you, God, the almighty Father,
in the unity of the Holy Spirit,
all honor and glory,
forever and ever.
Amen.

Memorial of His Death

An American who visits Volendam will naturally take
home with him a pair of wooden shoes. By doing so he
takes with him a little part of Holland.

After the war a priest who had spent some time in a
concentration camp met other people who had endured
the same afflictions as he. At this reunion the table was
beautifully set and the hall decorated festively. On the
table there was a white damask cloth, on which were
sparkling wine glasses and many white flowers. When the

first course was brought on the table, it formed a sharp contrast with the surroundings. It was a piece of stained, moldy bread, the same kind of bread they had eaten for years in the concentration camp. It was meant to be a reminder of the common bond they shared with each other. Yet at the moment that this bread was put on the table the reality of the past overwhelmed all of those present. The tablecloth vanished and became the wooden boards of the barracks. The flowers disappeared and the green decorations became barbed wire. The scent of the air turned into the stench of the barracks; everyone was seized with terror. The past had become present; the bread had brought it in. The bread was the meeting place of the past and the present. Naturally, to a stranger's eye nothing had changed in the room; but for those who had experienced the concentration camp everything had changed.

Does something like this happen in the eucharist? Yes, indeed, except for this: there the reality is more real; it is sacramental. On the last evening of his life Christ gave us a souvenir of himself, an inheritance, a memorial, but one which is more filled with reality than was the bread from the concentration camp.

When it is said that he was recognized in the breaking of the bread after his resurrection, we may assume that this term "the breaking of the bread" meant the eucharist, because in the Acts of the Apostles this expression is the technical term for the eucharist. It does not seem correct to us to see in this expression only the breaking of the bread. It connotes the whole, as does also our word "Mass." Strictly speaking, this word means the final dismissal; nonetheless, we also use this term for the whole celebration.

Thus we may presuppose that Jesus did for the two disciples on their way to Emmaus what he had done at the Last Supper. He broke the bread and said: "This is my body, given for you." At that moment their eyes were opened; they then saw the whole series of events come alive before them: the horrible night on which he had been betrayed, the day on which he had given himself wholly, on which his blood trickled down the cross as did the blood of the lamb on the doorposts of Egypt. "This is my blood, given for you." With eyes opened wide and in deathly silence they looked in amazement at the table where the holy bread lay and at the cup, while they remembered that night. And they saw it all again—the betrayal, the scourging, the death on the cross. Better than at the Last Supper, they now understood what Christ was doing. In the bread which he now handed them and gave to them they saw their master who had delivered himself to death for our redemption. They saw it all again, as though actually transpiring before their eyes.

The people at the reunion smelled again the stench of the concentration camp when they smelled the bread. The disciples of Emmaus experienced again the tension of the night of the passion when Christ handed them the bread. This should also happen to us when we are given the bread. To be sure we have the added difficulty that we were not there that night; our memory cannot help us as it did the disciples of Emmaus. But we have a reliable resort —the sacred scriptures. Whoever reads here with faith can participate in the past.

It will be helpful here to recall the prophecies of Isaiah concerning the servant of Yahweh. At the beginning of the eucharist obvious allusion is made to the following passage:

Behold, my servant shall prosper;
he shall be exalted and lifted up,
and shall be very high.
As many were astonished at him—
his appearance was so marred,

beyond human semblance,
and his form beyond that of the sons of men—
so shall he startle many nations;
kings shall shut their mouths
because of him.

For he grew up . . . like a young plant,
and like a root out of dry ground;
he had no form or comeliness
that we should look at him,
and no beauty that we should desire him.
He was despised and rejected by men;
a man of sorrows, and acquainted with grief;
he was despised as one from whom men hide their faces . . .
and we esteemed him not.

Surely he has borne our griefs
and carried our sorrows;
yet we esteemed him stricken,
smitten by God and afflicted.
But he was wounded for our transgressions;
he was bruised for our iniquities;
upon him was the chastisement that made us whole,
and with his stripes we are healed. . . .

He was oppressed, and he was afflicted,
yet he opened not his mouth;
like a lamb that is led to the slaughter,
and like a sheep that before its shearers is dumb,
so he opened not his mouth. . . .

By oppression and judgment he was taken away;
and as for his generation,
who considered that he was cut off
out of the land of the living,
stricken for the transgression of my people?
And they made his grave with the wicked
and with a rich man in his death,
although he had done no violence,

and there was no deceit in his mouth.
Yet it was the will of the Lord to bruise him.

He poured out his soul to death,
and was numbered with the transgressors;
yet he bore the sin of many,
and made intercession for the transgressors.

(Is. 52, 13-15; 53, 2-12)

In a piece of moldy, dark, hard bread, all the misery of a concentration camp again became present. This bread was the point of contact with the past.

The eucharist is even more the point of contact with the past. In the Mass, the memorial of the Lord, we have the point of contact with Calvary: the encounter with his death, the encounter with him *who delivered himself to death*. This association is more real than the association with the concentration camp. Here there was only an imperfect human symbol. But in the eucharist we have the perfect human symbol, the sacrament. Here we really encounter his death. Here everything is present, not only in an imperfect memorial, in imagery, but in sacramental reality.

Memorial of the Redemption

What we do in the Mass happened the first time during the Last Supper. It is well to remember that that day was the highlight of the Jewish paschal celebration. It was a national feast day on which the Jews commemorated the origin of their people, the birthday of the Jewish nation; it was the feast of liberation on which they solemnized and experienced anew their liberation from Egypt. When Christ was gathered with his disciples on that evening, he was undoubtedly filled with the same sentiments that possessed every Jew. The celebration of the feast was surrounded with many symbols; the underlying allusion of these symbols is rich in content. Christ adapted his banquet wholly to this background. Thus, if we want to understand the Last Supper and the Mass we must be acquainted with the profound symbolism of the Jewish paschal meal.

It is not necessary to describe this paschal meal in all its details. But it is important to know that on the table there were unleavened bread, bitter herbs, and a sort of sauce, the color of cement. There was also a lamb from which the blood had been drawn. All these objects naturally had their own symbolism. The bread was unleavened; it was not given time to raise. This reminded every Jew of the haste in leaving Egypt. The grey-yellowish sauce reminded them of the mud from which they had to make bricks during their enslavement. The lamb whose blood had been smeared on the doorposts had saved them from the angel of death, who on the night of the liberation went through Egypt and slew the firstborn.

We must imagine for ourselves how these symbols represented for them the reality of the slavery and the liberation. This meal was definitely different from the ordinary Jewish meal; the whole was enveloped in an atmosphere commemorating the liberation from slavery. Even today the youngest child in a Jewish family asks the father during this meal: "Father, why is this night different from all other nights? Why do we this night eat unleavened bread? Why do we eat bitter herbs?" Then the father begins to recount the story. He takes the bread in his hands and says: "This is the bread of affliction which our forefathers ate in Egypt." He permits those at table to taste the bitter herbs, and he urges his children to taste them well, because "in every generation every individual must look upon himself as having been freed from Egypt. How can anyone love freedom, unless he has tasted the bitterness of slavery?"

These words are self-explanatory and teach us much as we meet to celebrate our liberation in the Mass. At the paschal meal every good Jew sensed that he was the object of God's love and merciful intervention; he personally shared the intense, exuberant joy occasioned by the liberation. This was the way in which Christ conducted the Last Supper. Then, too, the youngest of the gathering (was it the apostle John?) put the question to the Lord: "Lord, why is this night so entirely different from all other nights? Master, why are we eating unleavened bread? Master, why do we eat bitter herbs?"

Then Jesus recalled the story, as did every other Jewish father to his family. He spoke of the liberation from Egypt. But what answer did Jesus give to the question why this night was so different from every other night and why this bread was being eaten? Did Jesus then say: "Because it is my body which will be given for you?" The apostles of Jesus certainly expected the exhortation which they had heard dozens of times at home: "Do this in memory of the liberation from Egypt and in memory of God's loving deeds." But here they received an entirely different answer: "Do this in memory of me."

In the Jewish Talmud it is written: "There will come a time when the exodus from Egypt will not be told anymore, to wit, when the second exodus, the second redemption, the great and final liberation will have been accomplished." These words have been fulfilled. Christ has eaten the bitter herbs with us; he has *become sin* for us. He wanted to share with us the misery of sin, but through this experience he brought us redemption. There is no eternal death anymore; we have the promised land in store. We are redeemed.

Here we must rely on our faith. Yet this faith has a human starting point. We know that Christ delivered himself for us. Because of this our minds must be filled with understanding when we hear him say: "This is my body, which is for you" (1 Cor. 11, 24). If one of our children should ask us: "Why is this meal so different from any other? Why do we eat this bread?" we can and must give the answer: "Because this bread is the body of the Lord, which he handed over for us."

Meal and Sacrifice

There is much discussion these days as to whether the Mass is a sacrifice, a banquet or a covenant. It seems to us best to begin by considering this problem from the aspect of the eucharist and from that of the Last Supper. Then we will at least come to see that it is basically a meal That it is also a covenant meal and a sacrifice will become more clear when we see the character of this meal.

Just what is a sacrifice? What does this word make us think of? What image do we evoke when we pronounce this word? A few examples will be helpful. A father has a very small income. He works as hard as he can, but his earnings remain meager. They barely suffice to feed his children. Yet in him there is a burning desire to give his children what other children receive. He is often over-whelmed by anguish that he cannot do this. But his poverty, his disregard of himself, his foregoing of things that he needs, such as his own desires for recreation and other things, finally make it possible for him to surprise his children just once. It is obvious that we are speaking of sacrifice. Many of us must perhaps admit that our parents were such, that they never had many pleasures in their lifetime, that they never permitted themselves any luxuries, that they did not take vacations and were constantly denying themselves things here and there to give us the chance to become what we are now. It is obvious; there was sacrifice here.

When healthy young men or beautiful young women

with a good deal of energy and vitality are moved by the spiritual needs of the world and consecrate themselves entirely as missionaries, then there is sacrifice. In its deepest sense sacrifice means giving oneself as a gift.

We know what constituted the sacrifice of Christ. We know how he gave himself really, unconditionally and wholly. He could truly say: "Greater love has no man than this, that a man lay down his life for his friends" (Jn. 15, 13). This is what he did in an absolutely perfect manner. It is as though he saw us when we were lost and separated from God, and as though he then recalled the words spoken at the dawn of creation: "It is not good that the man should be alone" (Gen. 2, 18). He came to us. In a certain sense he set aside his divine splendor and assumed the form of a slave. Yet not even this sufficed him. Like water he settled at the lowest point of our misery. He took our sins upon himself. On the cross he experienced the anguish of abandonment to such a degree that he cried out: "My God, my God, why hast thou forsaken me?" (Mt. 27, 46). This is the extent of his condescension; this is the degree of his solidarity with us. On the cross he utterly disregarded himself, he offered himself, he gave himself for us.

Isaiah had some prior inkling of this. In his Servant Songs he gives the moving description of the man of sorrows who surrendered himself to death for the welfare of others. Isaiah summarizes his prophecy in one sentence and this sentence describes the sacrifice of Christ: "He poured out his soul to death" (Is. 53, 12). Perhaps we ought to translate the original with the words: "He delivered his soul to death." It should be noted that Isaiah used the same words "given" and "delivered" that were used during the institution of the eucharist. There it is used twice. This surely is not accidental. Scripture scholars repeatedly call our attention to the literary connections between the Old and the New Testaments. The usage of the same words here was surely not lost on the apostles. They were acquainted with the scriptures; ninety-nine percent of their entire religious formation consisted in a knowledge of them. Unfortunately, in our day it is only a subordinate part of our formation. They surely noticed in the word "given" the allusion to the prophecy of Isaiah.

The words of institution speak of the "body which is given for you" (Lk. 22, 19ff.). The same word is used in describing the action of Christ: "He broke it and *gave* it to them" (Lk. 22, 19). Possibly we never recognized this special symbol in the distribution of holy communion or in the handing over of the bread. However, in view of these texts there is real symbolism. It expresses a surrender. Thus here, too, there is an allusion to sacrifice. In reality the Mass is a meal; yet this meal is a sacrifice because the host gives himself to men.*

* Ed. Note: In all of this, we must keep in mind the fact that the Eucharistic sacrifice is not just the offering of Jesus to us, his brethren. It is also, and most fundamentally, the offering of Jesus to the Father. Our sacrifice for each other and the sacrifice of Jesus for us draw their ultimate significance from the fact that the Son of God made flesh offered himself to the Father of us all. Thus, the Mass is not only the means by which we are more deeply reconciled to each other; it is also the means by which we are reconciled to God. The Mass is the means of human fraternity, it is true; but, it is also redemption, salvation, and atonement. It not only heals us by enabling us to love each other; but, it also becomes the means by which God loves us and we are able to love him.

We must, therefore, see the Mass not only as a meal, that is, in its vertical dimension by which we learn how to serve each other. We must see the Mass, furthermore, as a sacramental offering of the one Sacrifice of the cross, that is, in its horizontal dimension by which we learn how to serve God. The Mass does not only celebrate the depth and the joy of human community; it does not only inspire human friendship and sharing. It also brings us into the comunitarian life of the Trinity whereby we learn how to pray through the Son in the power of the Spirit, "Abba, Father". The Mass opens into the deepest dimensions of the sacred and speaks to us not only of brotherhood but also of God. It does all this because our brother Christ was also God's Son. It accomplishes all this because Jesus offered himself not only for us but in filial devotion to the Father of us all.

Food Is Given

We are inclined to view a meal, any meal, from only one aspect: we partake of it and we eat the food that has been prepared. Yet there is another aspect: we can eat the food only when it is given. This is the aspect we would like to focus on here because it plays an important role in the eucharist. To invite someone to a meal is an important and ancient human symbol. The bread in the mother's hand is different from that in the display window of the bakery. When a mother puts a little piece in the mouth of her child, this bread contains some of her care; in that act of giving is manifested her concern for the well-being of her child.

How actual this is can easily be shown by an example. A woman prepares a glorious meal for her husband on his birthday. She works at it for hours because she wants to surprise him. Everything looks wonderful; it has become something special. She is already anticipating the joy and appreciation as the various courses are served. How his eyes will open. Finally, the moment arrives when she serves the special dish. Smiling in anticipation, she steps from the dining room to the kitchen. She lifts the dish from the stove, slips and lets the whole preparation fall on the floor. Everything is ruined. She is inconsolable, not because of the food that has fallen on the floor, but because she dropped what was meant to be a token of her love for him. This bowl contained her love for him; now she is no longer able to manifest her appreciation in such a grandiose manner. It was precisely the presentation of this dish that was to express the greatness of her love.

When Christ says over the bread: "This is my body given for you," his whole love is contained in this bread. This bread is a symbol of his love; his outgoing concern is really contained in it. Yet there is more here than in the example of the woman. We have already mentioned that

Christ surrendered his life to death for us. When Christ approached the table for that last meal he was really approaching his deathbed. From the moment he handed the bread to his apostles he began taking leave of his life. The sacrifice which found its zenith on the cross begins here. It is here that he gives his life; his sacrifice begins in this act of giving. That is why he says that this is his body which will be "given."

It is obvious that the gesture of giving made by Christ is more symbolic than that made by the woman. We know that the sacrifice of Christ is present in the Mass. We hope that after this explanation this knowledge is no longer something vague, but that we see somewhat more clearly that Christ could not have presented his sacrifice better than as a meal. We should now realize that the distribution, or the handing over of the bread, is very important. This, too, contains its symbol of sacrifice, the symbol of this "giving of himself." The words used by Jesus to make his sacrifice present—"This is my body which is given for you"—are translated into action by the giving of food in communion.

From what has been said it should be clear that the distribution of holy communion is not something of a lower order; it should be done the way Christ himself did it. For those receiving holy communion this moment ought to be filled with holy reverence because here the Lord is giving himself entirely.

Given for Us

If there is one subject that the apostles in their preaching were not able to exhaust, it is the vicarious character of Jesus' passion. They were keenly aware that Christ died on the cross for us; he hung there as the representative of mankind. More than once they resort in their preaching to the words of Isaiah: "Ours were the 'sufferings he bore, ours the sorrows he carried. He was pierced through for our faults, crushed for our sins." These words made a deep impression on the apostles; it was a thought remaining uppermost in their minds. St. Peter says: "Christ also suffered for you, leaving you an example that you should follow in his steps. He committed no sin; no guile was found on his lips. When he was reviled, he did not revile in return; when he suffered, he did not threaten; but he trusted to him who judges justly. He himself bore our sins in his body on the tree" (1 Pet. 2, 21-24).

St. Paul says: "[Christ] gave himself for our sins to deliver us" (Gal. 1, 4); "[He] gave himself for us to redeem us" (Tit. 2, 14); "[He] loved me and gave himself for me" (Gal. 2, 20); "Walk in love, as Christ loved us and gave himself up for us" (Eph. 5, 2). In his first Epistle, John speaks in this same manner when he says: "By this we know love, that he laid down his life for us" (1 Jn. 3, 16). There are many more texts.

This vicarious character naturally has its consequences for us. When someone does something in my name, then I must agree with him. If someone pays a visit of condolence in our name, the natural assumption is that these are our feelings, that we are in accord with the action. The other person must have the assurance that we assent; otherwise the visit is a meaningless gesture. During the war when our young men fought in mortal danger for freedom, the thought which gave them courage and helped them through difficult moments was that we were giving them our gratitude and approval. Therefore, such agreement is surely demanded more than ever at the sacrifice of Christ, which is wholly vicarious. Whoever does not agree with it implicitly is excluded from salvation. Christ redeemed us but not without our cooperation. Christianity is not an automatic dispenser of salvation.

Thus it is not surprising that Christ asks us to express our agreement clearly. That is why he urges us to follow him in carrying our cross; that is why our readiness to sacrifice is asked especially in the eucharist, where he makes his sacrifice present. To receive holy communion is to identify oneself with the sacrificing Christ. That is why those who are present are asked to foster within themselves the same mind which was in Jesus Christ.

It is only natural that those present are asked to give a sign of their readiness to sacrifice, of their agreement with the sacrifice of the Lord. It is they who bring the bread and wine for the sacrifice; this serves as a symbol of what they feel. A similar sign of their charitable thoughts concerning the poor and the needy is contained in the collection; it is an indication that they want to have the same mind as Jesus had in giving his life for his own.

The Lord's Day

The eucharist is the memorial of the Lord. The day on which this memorial is celebrated is Sunday, the Lord's day. Sunday must have been very meaningful to the early Christians; they declared to their pagan judges that they could not live without Sundays. It is known that they kept secret from non-Christians what happened in their own assemblies on Sundays; it was a secret that was not even shared with the catechumens. One could only observe that the Christians assembled before dawn, but what they did was unknown. It was a secret. Yet they found these gatherings so important and so indispensable that there were people in times of persecution who exposed their lives to danger in order to be able to attend these gatherings. They literally risked their lives because they could not live without the Sunday. This is indeed a sharp con-

trast with what the Sunday actually means for many at
the present time. There are many people today to whom
Sunday spells boredom. It begins by sitting in a church,
waiting anxiously until the finish of a tedious obligation.
What was the high point of the week and an indispensable prop for the first Christians has become a dull necessity for many modern Christians. One often sees people
leaving church gaping and yawning with boredom. They
are only filled with derision when from the pulpit the
Mass is explained as the celebration of a feast. This
sounds ironic—and it is.

After sitting through this obligation there follows for
many a long, lonely and slowly passing day on which they
really do not know what to do. They may not dig in the
garden or decorate the room; in the course of time there
have been even serious disputes whether one might sew,
but not knit, or vice versa. What else is there left to do? If
it were not for sports, the situation would be utterly hope-
less. We might well ask what we have done with Sunday.
We have made dry and dull a day which should be glorious. The room which on Saturday evening seemed so
pleasant is so totally different on Sunday afternoon that
one can hardly stand it. To those who must work on Sunday because of social circumstances, the day is not at all
boring, but they discover that they have no Sunday. Sunday . . . and then work! It should be noted here that for the
early Christians Sunday was a normal working day; and
yet it was a real Sunday for them! Even in our day there
are many people for whom Sunday is a real feast day.
Among them certainly are the young people who are in
love; for them Sunday is a feast day to which they have
been looking forward all week because on that day they
can be together.

Is not this "being-together"—though in a deeper sense
than that noted above—the real meaning of Sunday? We

call this day "the Lord's day." In the Old Testament there is frequent mention of "the day of the Lord." It is the day on which the sovereign God would appear in all his majesty, on which he would manifest his power, subdue his adversaries and, above all, gather together his elect. Well then, Sunday is that day, because it was on Sunday that something happened that had never happened before. On that day Christ conquered death. This may sound like a cliché, but it is a weighty truth. On that day he appeared in all his glory, risen from the grave. On that day he gathered together his chosen people. "Go and tell my brethren to go to Galilee, and there they will see me" (Mt. 28, 10). This must be *the* day for all mankind. This day means that a man of this world is now in glory; one of us has risen. More than that, the head of all mankind has risen. This means that we will also share in glory, for the body follows the head. On this day proof was given to all mankind that Christ had really redeemed us from the horrible fate hanging over our heads—death as our final lot. We could not escape it of ourselves. We could not do a thing about it; we had to submit to it in an entirely passive manner. But on this day he freed us from death. He is obviously stronger than death; he is Lord over death.

On this day the early Christians gathered together, and they celebrated the eucharist. Then they knew that the Lord was present among them. As redeemed, they were gathered together with him.

As far as our *sentiments* are concerned, Christmas—or, in reference to Holy Week, Good Friday—remains the high point of the Church year. But Christmas and Good Friday would be meaningless if that Sunday had not followed. If Christ had not risen, the incarnation would have remained without meaning; if he had not risen, his suffering would not have made sense; if he had not risen, our faith would be vain and worthless. But he has risen; thus we gather together on Sunday to commemorate his work, his suffering, and especially his resurrection. And there is not a great deal of difference between thinking and thanking.

Until He Comes

We should not find it hard to imagine with what sentiments those who knew Christ celebrated the eucharist on Sundays. Their memory of the Lord was still so vivid; they had seen and experienced his divinity. Even we can sense this in the opening paragraph of St. John's first Epistle: "That which was from the beginning, which we have heard, which we have seen with our eyes, which we have looked upon and touched with our hands, concerning the Word of life . . . we proclaim also to you, so that you may have fellowship with us. . . . And we are writing this that our joy may be complete" (1 Jn. 1, 1-4).

Jesus' divinity so entranced them, so captivated them, that they were totally overwhelmed by it; it could not be otherwise. People like Mary Magdalene could only think and speak of one thing—the Lord's goodness. She had experienced it; she had knelt breathless and bewildered when the Lord had forgiven her many sins. It could not be otherwise with Peter who had betrayed the Lord but had been forgiven by him. He could only speak of the goodness of the Lord.

We can vividly imagine how these people celebrated the eucharist, how they proclaimed the reality of the death and the goodness and the resurrection of the Lord. St. John was so filled with the Lord that as an old man he could only repeat: "Love one another"; and when he was asked to say something else he knew only one answer: "But that is what the Lord said."

These people were literally possessed with an ineffable nostalgia for his second coming. They knew that he had risen; they knew also that he would come again. He himself had said: "And when I go and prepare a place for you, I will come again and will take you to myself, that where I am you may be also" (Jn. 14, 3). They were, so to speak, waiting for this event; they were continuously watching the door, because at some time the Lord might open it.

Whenever we celebrate the eucharist in our gatherings, we, too, do this in memory of him. This commemoration is not purely abstract; it is not a matter of fantasy. It is a lived memory, a commemoration filled with the presence of the Lord.

We know that the last gift given us by someone dear contains something of the dear one. A clock on the mantel, the wristwatch given as the final gift by one's mother —these are valued beyond gold, for they contain something of one's mother. The memorial of our Lord in the eucharist is more real than any of these examples. In this commemoration the Risen One lives on; he is present, truly present here. It is a remembrance of his passion, of his passover, of his ascension. Whoever celebrates this memorial for what it really is has the risen Lord standing before his eyes.

He is truly present. And yet we see only as in a dull mirror. We try to polish the mirror, but we are not wholly successful. We blink our eyes to sharpen our vision, but we cannot bring it into better focus. He is there, but shrouded in mystery. That is why this commemoration fills us with expectation. We look forward to his glorious, unveiled coming. Of this we are certain: we shall see his goodness in all its resplendent beauty. We shall see him in his glorious, outgoing love.

During the celebration of the eucharist we look forward with confidence to the moment when we may eat and drink with him in God's kingdom. Our assurance is based on his own word. He said so. He went to his Father and in his Father's house there are many rooms; he went to prepare a place for us. We can no longer have any doubt about it. Thus the celebration of the eucharist is an exhortation to us to remain awake, to stand ready, because he may come when we are not expecting him.

This has not happened yet; we are still waiting. We celebrate his memory "until he comes." At that time we will no longer see vaguely as in a mirror, but face to face. Then faith and hope will disappear, and only love will remain. Then we will be united with the Lord forever.

We Are Still Wayfarers

"Wanderer" is a word that does not appear often in our present-day speech. The only place where we find it is in the scriptures. It should be noted that this word occurs for the first time in reference to Abraham when he leaves his country at God's request and goes to a strange land (Deut. 26, 5). Then he is a wayfarer. The word means to be a stranger, to have no settled dwelling place or civic rights, to be a pilgrim. A wanderer is one who moves about from place to place. When Abraham was en route, he was a stranger; he had no settled domicile, no right of citizenship; he was a traveler, a pilgrim. The Jews, too, were wanderers when they journeyed in the desert on their way to the promised land; at that time they were strangers.

This seems to be a fundamental thought in salvation history. Time and again people are reminded that they must behave themselves as wanderers in this world. This idea is so important that God reminds the Jews of it constantly. When the Jews feel too much at home in the land which they possess, when they forget that all this is only a token, God compels them to rediscover the notion of being wanderers. He permits them to be led away to the concentration camps in Assyria and Babylon. There they discover that they are wanderers, a people *en route*.

This must be the basic attitude of Christians, too. When one loses sight of this, his Christian life loses its savor. We must be constantly aware that although we live in this world and have a duty and a commission to perform here, the part of our lives that we are living at the present is a passing one. This world must still be perfected. Christians are therefore not despisers of this world, but builders. Estrangement from the world is not Christian. The world is God's creature and his gift, but this world is *en route* with us to a new world. In its present state it is still unfinished, incomplete, and thus not our definitive dwelling place.

No wonder that the first pope, Peter, reminds his Christians of this and urges: "Beloved, I beseech you as aliens and exiles to abstain from the passions of the flesh that wage war against your soul" (1 Pet. 2, 11). St. Clement addressed his Christians in like manner: "The Church of God residing [as strangers] at Rome."

Here we have the basic reason why we never feel fully at home in this world, why we can never be entirely happy here. We have been created for another world. This presupposes that in a certain sense we must be different from people who do not have this mentality. It is obvious that people living only for this world and expecting their full happiness here, who know no future, no hereafter, who do not believe in a new world in heaven, arrive at a sort of materialism. Does not Paul have them say: "Let us eat and drink; tomorrow we shall be dead"?

For us, however, things are different. Because we know that this life is only a transitional phase, we live with a certain detachment. Thus it is not strange that among us there are people who voluntarily live in poverty, chastity and obedience to be symbols to the world that there is yet a different world to come. Another hallmark of wayfarers is that they support each other. We are en route as a people, as a community. Therefore no one may be left behind; therefore there must be a great sense of fellowship. No one may be lost in solitude; we must remain together. That is why we gather together to celebrate the eucharist. The eucharist is the hallmark of this passing state; we shall celebrate the eucharist "until he comes." Through the celebration of the eucharist we wait with intense longing and expectation for that moment in which the Lord shall take us to that land where God himself will wipe the tears from our eyes, where there will be no weeping, no sorrow, no death, where he will make all things new. As long as we have not reached this land which eye has not seen, which ear has not heard, and which no human mind had been able to imagine, we regard ourselves as wayfarers; we are people en route.

Wanderers have yet a third characteristic. They are en route under the leadership of Christ. He was the wayfarer par excellence because he came into this world from the Father. He left this world to go to the Father, but he went to prepare a place for us there, because, as he assured us, in his Father's house there are many rooms. He is the one who goes ahead. In the desert the Jews were led by a column of light, and Christ said: "I am the light of the world; he who follows me will not walk in darkness" (Jn. 8, 12). He is the one who leads the way and takes us by the hand. It is at Mass that this becomes a living reality and we experience it.

As Moses was the prophet for the wandering Jewish people and proclaimed God's Word to them, so Christ stands before us in the eucharist as the one to whom we must listen. Christ himself called attention to this when he quoted from the old law: "It was said to the men of old, 'You shall not kill. . . .' But I say to you: . . . whoever says 'You fool!' shall be liable to the hell of fire" (Mt. 5,

22ff.). In his Gospel he perfects the Jewish law; he is the new Moses, of whom the Father said: "Listen to him."

Yahweh let the water spring from a rock to quench the thirst of his wandering people; but Christ is the living water, and whoever drinks from it shall never be thirsty again (Jn. 4, 13). Yahweh fed the hungry people in the desert by letting manna fall from heaven; in the eucharist Christ is the bread that comes from heaven: "Your fathers ate the manna in the wilderness, and they died. . . . If anyone eats of this bread, he will live forever" (Jn. 6, 49-51).

Thus to be a wanderer is the hallmark of the Christian. We are en route under the leadership of the Lord. In the eucharist we are aware of being a pilgrim people, we seek mutual support and love, and we experience the leadership of the Lord. That is why we are wayfarers especially at Mass; it is precisely at the eucharist that we are encouraged as pilgrims and strangers on this earth to keep ourselves from fleshly lusts which war against the soul.

We are people with an eye to the future. That is why we pray: "Come, Lord Jesus!" (Apoc. 22, 20).

Conclusion

It will be a long time and a far journey before liturgy and life will meet fully. The difference between the two has become too great. However, we may not expect them ever to meet unless we ourselves prepare for it. We notice on all sides how efforts are being made to bring the Church and the world together. The development and deepening of theological thought is clear proof of this. No less a proof is the argumentation which took place at Vatican Council II concerning the many problems facing the Church. In spite of difficulties and opposition, in spite of the activities of particular people who are not sympathetic toward us, in spite of disappointments, we must say that our Church is making every effort to become human again as Christ was human. In a certain sense what happened at Vatican Council II happened 2,000 years ago. Then God became man; he appeared not as a superhuman being but as *the* fellowman par excellence. He came neither with power and majesty nor as a dictator, and certainly not as one prepared to condemn. He came with an extraordinary, almost incredible, understanding of the man in the world. This is what we now see happening in the Church. She is striving to become human again, and to understand the man in the world. She wants to be the bride of Christ, without spot or stain. That is why she subjects herself to a merciless self-criticism, for it is certain that the Lord who is so perfectly human cannot choose a bride who is not human, who has no concept of the needs of men, no eye for the world in which she lives. God came into the world; his Church may not remain outside it.

It is always dangerous to use the word "Church" if we are not conscious of *being* the Church. Without this consciousness there is the danger of using the word as something abstract, something far removed, something intangible, something one can blame easily because he does not then feel himself reprimanded. Without this awareness one may indeed expect everything from the Church, but it will be a senseless expectation, since no one will endeavor to fulfill it. If we were to speak thus about the Church, the Church would be as impersonal as the nondescript "one." Whoever says: "*Someone* will take care of it," or "*Some* say," or "*Some* blame," is actually speaking about no one. We must be conscious of the fact that *we* are the Church. Then it will become more difficult but more meaningful to blame the Church, because then the accusations will be leveled at ourselves. Then also will it be more difficult but more meaningful to expect much of the Church because then *we* will be responsible for the fulfillment of that expectation.

It is we, therefore, who must arrange and bring about the convergence of liturgy and life. This is a task not only for Vatican Council II and the post-conciliar commission for the liturgy; it is a task for all of us.